To Steve,

Sometimes in your business you need to "ladda".

Enjoy!

Eric V. Holtz

M000199010

Laddering

Laddering

Unlocking the Potential of Consumer Behavior

Eric V. Holtzclaw

WILEY

Cover image: Michael J. Freeland
Cover design: © Anthony Harvie/Digital Vision/Jupiter Images

Copyright © 2013 by Eric V. Holtzclaw. All rights reserved.

Published by John Wiley & Sons, Inc., Hoboken, New Jersey.
Published simultaneously in Canada.

Illustrations by Kaitlyn Holtzclaw

For general information about our other products and services, please contact our Customer Care Department within the United States at (800) 762-2974, outside the United States at (317) 572-3993 or fax (317) 572-4002.

Wiley publishes in a variety of print and electronic formats and by print-on-demand. Some material included with standard print versions of this book may not be included in e-books or in print-on-demand. If this book refers to media such as a CD or DVD that is not included in the version you purchased, you may download this material at http://booksupport.wiley.com. For more information about Wiley products, visit www.wiley.com.

Library of Congress Cataloging-in-Publication Data:

Holtzclaw, Eric, V., 1973–
    Laddering: Unlocking the Potential of Consumer Behavior/Eric V. Holtzclaw.
      pages cm.
    ISBN: 978-1-118-56612-1 (cloth); ISBN: 978-1-118-65297-8 (ebk);
    ISBN: 978-1-118-65357-9 (ebk)
      1. Consumer behavior. I. Title.
    HF5415.32.H637   2013
    658.8′342—dc23

2013008506

Printed in the United States of America

10 9 8 7 6 5 4 3 2 1

To my girls:

April, who is always my greatest cheerleader and my unwavering constant.

Kaitlyn, who is both the reflection of who I am and the example of whom I aspire to be.

Contents

Preface

The only constant is change, continuing change, inevitable change, that is the dominant factor in society today. No sensible decision can be made any longer without taking into account not only the world as it is, but the world as it will be.

—Isaac Asimov

I LOVE TO travel. It's the ultimate way to support my underlying need and desire for change—a new location every day, a new city to experience, new cuisine to try. My future self has no permanent address or day-to-day responsibilities. The world is a huge, ever-changing place that's just too enticing for me to refuse. I absolutely must explore it, understand it, and consume it.

Until I can afford to hang it all up and travel the world endlessly, I have built a career that has supported my core need for something new, something different. The companies I have built or helped build have covered a wide range of industries and products. This experience has granted me a unique perspective and made me an expert witness to the dramatic and disruptive changes technology has had on how individuals work, live, play, and interact.

Unlike the typical stereotype of technically oriented people—who desire only to work heads down on coding or building something cool or new—I view technology as an enabler, a way to make life better and more efficient. I knew very early in my career that I wanted to understand both the technology as well as how its use affected or changed the world. But even with this slightly more open attitude toward technology, I still had a blind spot.

I thought I knew what my consumers needed. After all, I had been trained and educated on how to implement technology to meet a problem; they hadn't. I was surrounded by other smart individuals who had equal or better experience deploying technology to consumers. What could we possibly be missing?

My passion for seeing technology from the users' perspective was solidified in 1995. It was the first time I was ever in a lab like the one at User Insight. I was working for a company called Information America, a division of West Publishing. We were a skunkworks who'd been commissioned to take an outdated mainframe system that allowed electronic access to public record information to the Internet. (I kiddingly say it was the first nonporn website on the Internet that was actually making money.)

We were about a week from launch when the marketing manager suggested we take the product through something she called usability testing. As a computer science geek at heart, I thought she was crazy. What could the *user* know about a system that our incredibly intelligent team didn't? I believed that the organizations supporting or selling the product needed to understand the technology, but I couldn't quite wrap my head around how the user could provide any meaningful direction.

I went along with this idea because I honestly thought it would help the marketing manager out more than me. She was interested in understanding what most marketers would care about with this type of product:

- What messages would resonate with consumers to make them use this new service?
- How much were they willing to pay to search for or retrieve a record?
- What concerns would they have about providing their financial or personal information?

So I begrudgingly agreed to play along in order to help *her* out—but threatened that it better not impact my precious timeline. As someone who always makes the dates in my project plans, I was concerned this distraction might derail our launch date.

The experience was very much like what you see on a television show when detectives interrogate a suspect and try to get them to admit to committing whatever crime is being investigated. My team sat huddled in a dark room behind one-way glass and watched a moderator take a consumer through a set of predefined tasks. They ranged from activities as simple as reviewing the site to understand what purpose it might serve to those that were a bit more complicated, allowing users to actually register and submit a search to see how they interpreted the results returned.

Fifteen minutes into the first user session, I was hooked—and my world had been changed forever.

The poor user couldn't even figure out how to enter his registration information. He failed at understanding how to submit payment information, he didn't know how to execute a search or interpret the results when they came back, and he wasn't even sure how to start over when he made it down a path that didn't meet his expectations.

In other words, it was a fantastic, beautiful failure.

The failure continued throughout the day as one consumer after another suffered through the same issues that the first had. My team started to desperately plea with them through the glass to "click that button" or "just scroll down." At one point, I was trying to send telepathic messages to the individual to help end his suffering in trying to properly enter his credit card information. I remember saying out loud (and being reprimanded by the facilitator because he was afraid the consumer would hear me), "Just look at the example; it's showing you that you need to break it up into sections. Why can't you see it?"

We had made the classic mistake of placing the submit button just below the fold. As a result, the primary designer kept repeating, almost as if she had lost her mind, "Just scroll down; just scroll down."

But no matter how much we tried to will the users from our darkened control center, they never learned. Each new user confirmed the system's overarching issues—and often pointed out something new that we didn't expect but needed to know.

My team walked out of that dark, cold room on a sugar high after consuming way too many M&M's, gummy bears, and salty snacks. We were not in a state of despair, as you might expect; rather, we had a developed sense of humility and a renewed passion for fixing this product. We wanted our consumers to understand what we were trying to provide and wanted to remove the barriers that were getting in their way. An unintended but positive consequence of every experience we had in lab was a renewed team spirit.

This evaluation was one of the best team-building experiences I have ever taken a team through. For the companies who come through our process and take it seriously, I see it bond them in a way no corporate retreat or motivational speaker could ever accomplish. It's especially amazing and fulfilling to watch individuals—many who have never met in person but work on the same product—introduce themselves in the lab and view what they have built through the eyes of a completely unbiased judge, a judge who can make or break the success of their efforts.

This initial experience did something incredibly crucial for me and my career. It opened my eyes to how important it was to look at whatever I was building from the perspective of the *person who is intended to use* the product. I immediately knew that if I was ever given the opportunity to create a company that worked in this area, I would jump at the chance. Eventually, it *did* lead me—along with my two cofounders—to build a company that became one of the fastest, highest-quality research companies in the world. We shepherded some of the largest companies and leading brands through the process of looking at their marketing and product development problems through their consumers' lens.

The company that spawned from this early experience is User Insight, which conducts 150 research projects a year across 30 different industries and works with some of the world's leading brands to understand why the products, services, and experiences they build work or don't work. It is the ultimate laboratory for exploring the intersection of the human with technology. As cliché as it sounds, the world has changed, and I have had the chance to watch this change happen from the consumer's perspective.

Over the course of just one decade, the world's focus shifted, from selling what could be produced (mass production) to asking the people consuming the product, technology, and marketing message (mass customization) what *they want.*

The changes have happened so quickly, dramatically, and permanently that few people with whom I talk truly understand the impact. We are essentially numb to advances in technology. We have gone from being excited by the newest technological advance to expecting and quickly absorbing the "next big thing" into our ecosystem. And we give very little thought to how far-reaching the implications these new advances will have on the world in which we live.

I remember signing up for one of the first bill paying services in the mid-1990s. It took forever to get the bill set up in the first place, not to mention that the company was still cutting a check and actually sending it to the biller. I can remember telling my friends and family excitedly about this new way to pay bills. I knew that this was a significant transformation in the way financial services and end consumers would interact with one another moving forward, a noticeable and understood disruption. I was willing to overlook the inefficiency of this new system in order to participate.

If it takes longer than a few seconds to pay a bill nowadays, we are annoyed. The conversations and presentations at a recent payment conference I attended centered on how consumers would soon be able to pay for items without even taking their phone out of their pocket at a local coffee shop or restaurant. This is the new norm; it's not considered earth-shattering, even if it is a dramatic departure from how commerce has been transacted in person to date.

An amazing amount of disruptive technology has been introduced over the past 20 years. I have had the unique opportunity to participate as an observer to and an agent of this disruption—a witness to how it has been implemented, why it's important, and what the impact has been on the average consumer.

Personal computers, cell phones, the Internet, MP3 players, smartphones, apps, and social media are just a *few* of the more memorable advances that have become commonplace. And with each new advancement and related disruption, the environment has changed forever. Humans are resilient; they accept these changes and move on. This is one of our greatest assets—and the reason we sit at the top of the evolutionary pyramid. But as a result, we rarely stop to take an audit of what these changes mean; how they have, in turn, changed *us*; and how they influence the way we interact with the world around us.

The recent disruption that all of this technology has caused at such an amazing pace—as well as their reduced costs—have forever changed the development of all products, services, and experiences. As a result, product development and marketing must also make a substantial modification to the way they approach their jobs.

This most recent set of disruptions and advances has led to the long prophesied "rise of the individual."

The point of this book is to synthesize conversations I've had and have overheard over the past few years into a sense of awareness, awakening and a change of focus to what's *really* important. Marketing and product development teams need the same wake-up call I received on that first day of usability testing in the mid-1990s. They must focus on their consumer and see their marketing messages and products through the consumers' eyes. Only then will relational marketing work and be implemented correctly.

The norms, and even industries, that we held true just a few short years ago no longer exist. This fallout is the direct result of focusing too much on what has worked in the past and not enough on what we need to do in the future. We must take a look at how we are building products, creating marketing messages, and determining the way forward differently than before.

The world is no longer operating according to business as usual. And without a realization of this change and a different approach moving forward, many more companies and industries are going to go the way of CDs, Blockbuster video stores, and Borders bookstores. Consumers are choosing the brands that understand and support them on an individual level, engage them through an authentic relationship, and give them what they want in the form that they want it.

The goal of the techniques I propose in this book—and practice in my work—is to accept and understand people for who they are, at whatever stage, personal or professional, they happen to be. I aim to understand how to talk to them at this core level to create a brand, experience, or service that meets their unique needs. And you should, too.

Companies need to learn how to thrive and accept the fragmentation that has occurred, not resist it. It's not about one message or product; it's about the *right* message or product. Companies must learn to support the individual as an individual and stop treating all customers like everyone else or treating them like they're part of a group into which they may not self-select.

The big secret is that the *core* of a consumer rarely changes; it takes a life event, not a life stage to dramatically affect the consumer's basic drivers. They simply manifest their core differently in different contexts or suppress it based on other influencers. Companies that expend the time and effort to truly understand this core instead of guessing or assuming are the ones who win. They become the brands everyone envies in our new relationship-driven, many-to-many economy.

And once you understand the core, the technology no longer matters. It becomes secondary. You view every product, marketing, or experience decision from the point of view of the constant: the consumer's DNA.

As a practitioner of laddering, it's important to me to explain how we got to where we are today. The first part of this book explains the rules we as marketers and product developers followed until just recently, why we followed them, and why, until just recently, they worked.

We are currently experiencing one of the most life- and industry-transforming periods of technology to date. You will find as you read through this book that each time a new disruption occurs, you must take time to review how it has affected the end consumer you are targeting or learn that the consumer you are targeting is no longer appropriate to your brand.

For those people who like change like I do, it's one of the coolest times to be in the marketing and product development space. It's time to create new rules, new ways of doing business and measuring success. And the very cool thing is that the secret to being successful in this endeavor is to do something that's so basic to each of us as human beings that we have forgotten how to do it: we need to **understand one another**.

Laddering will teach you how to do just that.

1

History

Advertising has us chasing cars and clothes, working jobs we hate so we can buy shit we don't need.
                                        —*Tyler Durden*, Fight Club, *1999*

Edward Bernays

It's a cold day in New York City in December 1918. World War I has just ended. Twenty-seven-year-old Edward Bernays ducks into a local drugstore to buy a Coca-Cola. As he sits at the pharmacy counter and enjoys his soft drink, he contemplates the new career he is about to begin. Edward is on the verge of a vocation that will impact the very product he's enjoying—in addition to countless others that sit on the shelves of that drugstore and many other stores in the years to come.

Edward, the nephew of Sigmund Freud, has just completed an assignment working for the war effort as a part of the Committee on Public Information, a group that was instrumental in promoting the American dream of democracy across the world. After many failed attempts to enlist and help out with the war effort, flat-footed and nearsighted Edward finally landed a chance to serve. He managed to secure an interview after his dogged pursuit of Ernest Poole, the head of the Foreign Press Bureau of the US Committee on Public Information. During his tenure with the committee, Edward worked with companies such as Ford, International Harvester, and many other American firms to distribute literature on US war efforts to foreign contacts and by posting US propaganda in the windows of 650 American offices overseas.

Edward's contributions to the Committee on Public Information helped make American citizen's perception of what had been an unpopular war much more positive. He used techniques he had successfully mastered in prior endeavors, including promoting a play called *Daddy Long Legs* and working with a touring ballet called Ballets Russe.

As a result of his work, Edward was invited to travel with Woodrow Wilson and attend the Paris Peace Conference in January 1919.

3

During his time abroad, Edward witnessed firsthand how powerful propaganda could be in influencing the general public's belief systems. This experience further convinced him that one could indeed shape the behavior of the masses by understanding what instincts and symbols motivate individuals. Edward explained, "The impact words and pictures made on the minds of men throughout Europe made a deep impression on me. I recognized that they had been powerful factors in helping win the war. Paris became a training school without instructors, in the study of public opinion and people."

And as it turned out, Edward's schooling and realization couldn't have come at a more opportune time.

The Problems of Production

Although the United States had left the war in a state of euphoria—and with the status of being the most powerful, richest country in the world—the country was facing several problems. American companies had perfected the practice of mass production primarily out of necessity to keep up with the demands of the war effort. Now that the war was over, they needed a way to maintain their prominence with this new capability. As such, they needed to address two problems, the first of which was that *these companies needed someone to buy their products.*

Before the ability to create products in mass was perfected, purchasers of goods were not referred to as consumers. This word comes from the Latin term *consumo* and means to "eat up completely." Prior to the war, people bought only what they needed, primarily locally. Only the very wealthy participated in conspicuous consumption. Therefore, the definition of what an individual needed had to change to support mass production.

Consumerism and the concept of a consumer were invented in part to support and perpetuate the mass production cycle. Richard

Robbins, in his book *Global Problems and the Culture of Capitalism*, explained it this way[1]:

> [T]he consumer revolution of the late nineteenth and early twentieth centuries was caused in large part by a crisis in production; new technologies had resulted in production of more goods, but there were not enough people to buy them. Since production is such an essential part of the culture of capitalism, society quickly adapted to the crisis by convincing people to buy things, by altering basic institutions and even generating a new ideology of pleasure.

The second problem was that *in order to mass produce something, choice must be limited.* Henry Ford is famously quoted as saying the following when discussing the Model T in 1909: "Any customer can have a car painted any color that he wants, so long as it is black."

For mass production to work, a product had to be standardized; nothing could be handmade, and everything had to be manufactured via machines and molds. The product's assembly must permit workers with low skill levels to operate assembly lines where each worker does one task over and over again. For instance, a Model T assembly worker might spend every day putting the same screws into the same part of the vehicle chassis.

The introduction of variety or choice would require time to retool a very expensive process, or even more daunting—to create a whole *new* assembly line to take on the new work. The technology at the time simply didn't exist to support the concept of choice.

---

[1] Richard Robbins, *Global Problems and Culture Capitalism* (Boston: Allyn & Bacon, 1999), 210.

The Opportunity

Edward and others in his industry saw both of these problems as an opportunity to apply the principles of propaganda in a completely new way. They believed that propaganda could serve to move society from one of need to one of *want*. Furthermore, they believed that using the right symbols, words, and influences could convince consumers to buy the products that companies were creating.

Edward knew that he couldn't use the word *propaganda* itself because it had been tainted by the Germans during the war. So he opened up a *publicity direction* office, which became what we now all know as public relations. This new office's charter was to *create* demand for the products companies were already making—and to find ways to expand a product's reach to new consumers.

Edward believed that if they approached customers the right way, those working in *publicity direction* could actually adjust the customers' preferences—and get them to consume what an industry was already creating.

One example of this approach is the way in which Edward handled American brewers. The brewers hired him after prohibition was repealed in 1933 to put themselves in a stronger position than liquor makers.

To create demand for beer among those who usually indulged in alcoholic beverages, Edward touted beer as the "beverage of moderation." It was an attempt to distance it from distilled liquor and set it apart as distinctive. He persuaded beer retailers to cooperate with law enforcement to ensure that their product was used responsibly, and he published evidence that beer was not fattening and had a caloric value equal to that of milk.

To expand the product's reach to new consumers, Edward told homemakers that beer would make for richer chocolate cake. He told farmers that brewers were major buyers of their barley, corn, and rice and told laborers that beer was the one alcoholic beverage they could afford. In addition, he published booklets and wrote letters claiming that beer was the favorite drink of the ancient Babylonians and the monks of the Middle Ages, as well as of George Washington, Thomas Jefferson, Patrick Henry, and the Pilgrims.

Edward's work affected products across the board, from hairnets to automobiles to cigarettes to even people. Politicians called on his services to help them move their campaigns forward. His approach was always similar: make people want to consume the product as it was presented or how it could be manufactured.

Edward primarily used the printed word to persuade individuals that they needed to buy a product. The advertisements were directive: they told the consumer *what* to buy.

- "Isn't it time you gave <u>yourself</u> a Christmas Gift?" (advertisement for a Colt revolver)
- "Christmas morning she will be happier with a Hoover" (advertisement for Hoover vacuum)
- "How Television Benefits Your Children"; "Own a Motorola and You <u>Know</u> You Own the Best" (advertisement for Motorola television set as a advertorial)
- "For a better start in life, start cola early" (advertisement for the Soda Pop Board of America)

And the approach was very effective: companies did succeed in getting individuals to buy what the company could manufacture.

The Rise of Mass Media

Edward Bernays and his cohorts' efforts received support from an invention whose advancement was just as important as mass production at the time: the rise of mass media.

Before the early 1900s, most people got their news and information via word of mouth. They heard about things when they visited the town square or from a sparsely distributed network of newspapers when they were out and about buying the things they needed. Technology to send messages cheaply wide and far didn't exist.

But the introduction of new disruptive technology in the early 1900s—such as the telephone, radio, movies, and television—greatly enhanced people's ability to send information, entertainment, and news directly into the household from a central location. Those who were able to afford to do this had a set number of channels, and these discrete channels allowed them to closely control what was said and how it was said.

However, not everyone had this luxury. Only large players with deep pockets could fund the entertainment and information to distribute across these channels. As a result, channel owners needed the advertiser to help support their endeavors. A symbiotic relationship developed—a long-standing institution of which we've begun to see fractures only recently.

The kind of control and distribution power that mass media held was perfect for sending the advertisers' messages intended to drive consumer demand for a given product or service.

Keeping Up with the Joneses

The country that came out of World War II was one composed of citizens who were accustomed to skimping by to support the war effort. Once the war was over, people had the money to spend on things they wanted—and the freedom to do so. The economic and societal environment of that time helped move the consumerism trend forward. Creating consumer demand continued to evolve in a way that further bolstered the burgeoning industry of public relations and advertising and reinforced the belief that advertisers were in charge. The consumer was a pawn, willing to purchase what was created as long as it was positioned with the right spin.

The government helped, too. To encourage spending, the government began doling out cheap money via the GI Bill to anyone that wanted a house. Suddenly, the American dream was within most people's grasp. Cities and towns everywhere began building affordable housing. Transportation systems were constructed to and from the city that made it easy for families to move out to the suburbs.

This was a society where people lived near others "like them"; in this way, neighborhoods truly did represent the groups in which they *decided* to live. Block parties were common, kids played with their neighborhood friends, and the influences of social hierarchy impacted which products and services people chose to buy.

The avenues through which these consumers received information were very closely controlled. In those days, you couldn't skip through commercials, you had very few channels, there was no Internet, and you spent substantial time with your neighbors. It was easy in this type of situation (which lasted well into the 1990s) to create an environment that made people feel as though they had to "keep up with the Joneses"—in other words, buy the things their neighbors were buying. It was practical for companies to view this society through a wide lens of demographics and segmentation—and to use these divisions to appeal to the various audiences.

Based on social pecking order, work's structure and rhythm, and a desire to fit in, the next big thing depended largely on placement and whether the right group or person liked it enough to make it sell. Use the right promotion, change a tagline, increase or decrease the price, and you could watch the numbers of units sold go up or down almost instantly.

Product Was Tangible; Information Was Scarce

Unlike today, another important difference back then was that people were mostly buying *tangible* items. They were *products*, and you had to *visit the store* to purchase them—an undertaking that required quite a bit of effort and commitment. Consumers needed to understand the features and functions of the item they were buying to ensure they were selecting the right product for them.

This meant that consumers were influenced by what they saw others doing, reading, or using. It required no effort to find out what books your friends or colleagues thought were interesting because you could see them carrying the books around. You could tell what music they were listening to because the record sleeves were mobile advertisements for the artists they contained.

Consumers didn't have many resources of information available to understand the difference between products, and what they did have was scarce, was hard to obtain, and often came with an associated cost either in terms of time or money. They relied heavily on feature and function comparison to determine which product or offering was most appropriate to them. The commitment to making a purchase was therefore far greater—and the consequences of making a "choice" all the more critical.

As a result, consumers were forced to rely heavily on what they saw in mass media—and what the store's friendly salesperson told them about any distinctions between available products. It was a marketer's job to get consumers to the store and the salesperson's task to establish a relationship with them. The retailer garnered the consumers' trust and advised them in selecting the right choice based on their needs.

In this distribution model, one that the seller highly controlled and maintained, sales was the quarterback, responsible for moving the consumer across the goal line. And the marketing department was the cheerleader, the creator of utopian messages about how a product or brand could make life better. The process was simple: whatever company did the best job at promoting its unique functions or features won. Consumers bought the product because of a halo effect around this set of features and functions. They truly believed that they would attain some higher order by buying a product, that they would fit in with their neighbors, have more free time, be a better wife or mother, or achieve whatever their goal or perceived unmet need happened to be.

Population Was on the Rise

Starting with the baby boomers (those born between the years of 1946 and 1964), people began to receive better educations. This meant higher-paying jobs and a growth in home ownership, a mass production economy's dream. The demand for things such as diapers, baby food, furniture, and appliances skyrocketed as more and more people purchased homes and welcomed new additions to the family.

Around this time, companies perfected the distribution methods they used to get products into stores. Marketing departments could begin to see firsthand the direct impact their efforts had on the buying behaviors of the consumers they were targeting. They could look at what had worked before, model it, and use this historical reference to predict future consumer purchases. This type of economy made it possible for giants like Walmart to refine the supply chain. They were able to measure exactly how much product to put on the shelves and what to price it at and could predict how it would sell.

These were the golden years of marketing and advertising. Run a commercial that a cereal helps with weight loss and watch the product fly off the shelf. Introduce a new toy with just the right message, and it becomes the must-have item of the holiday buying season. Present an advertisement about what success looks like and influence the trends in boardrooms across America.

Customization and the "Experience Economy"

However, fractures began to appear in this mass production model's framework as we moved into the 1990s. Companies such as Dell made it possible for consumers to build a computer exactly the way they wanted it. The Internet threatened to turn us all into basement-dwelling, sun-avoiding, online shoppers who never wanted to venture out of our homes for fear of being cut from the tether of our online connections.

The Internet helped spawn something that came to be known as the *experience economy*. Consumers started expecting more from brands than just a good product. In fact, getting a good product was only the starting point; they wanted something more, something different. The Internet provided access to information about different products and services that consumers had never had before.

Mass media was not affected negatively by the experience economy; if anything, most mass media players were bolstered. In these early days of the Internet, it was expensive to capitalize on this new channel, just as it had been during the introduction of radio, television, and movies. Most of the information was still tightly controlled and delivered via large corporate websites or aggregators. That's when smart companies, such as Amazon, started using service and experience as a way to differentiate themselves from others.

I remember the chief executive officer (CEO) of the company I was working for in the mid-1990s excitedly talking about how responsive Amazon was after he placed an order. He gushed about how they'd sent him e-mails that let him know when the book he had ordered would ship (back when Amazon was just an online bookstore). In the beginning, Amazon added small perks; they upgraded shipping from ground to next day or sent some type of bonus with your order. As a result, these "little things" started to permeate the buying public's psyche. The time eventually came when it was no longer enough merely to *receive* the product you ordered in good condition. Companies had to offer something better—and the easiest element to affect was their experience in receiving the product. In these early days, the Internet merely bolstered mass production channels.

Consumers now expected little perks, which gave rise to a variety of new business models. One of the most popular was that embraced by online retailer Zappos, which allowed its buyers to buy as much apparel—and make as many requests—of their customer support reps as they wished. They have a very liberal return policy, allowing consumers to "experience" their products and decide which to keep and which to return.

Not every new business had success with this approach. Webvan was a failed grocery delivery service that brought groceries to your doorstep and prided themselves on the experience they provided. Their goal was to deliver the best produce, add perks to every order and go out of their way to make sure consumers would order from them again. If Webvan hadn't taken on too much infrastructure when it attempted to recreate an entire well-established distribution model on a low-margin business, it could be the way we all receive our groceries today. Webvan was too far ahead of the mass customization curve.

Of course, the examples cited here of companies attempting this move toward an experience economy were all taking place online. But the impact was also occurring offline. People became more willing to buy commodity items at a higher price if they were wrapped in some kind of heightened experience. Gilmore and Pine note coffee as a great example of this shift in their 1999 book *The Experience Economy*.

No matter how much some us love coffee, it *is* really just a commodity. And as a commodity, it is sold at a rate of about 1 cent per cup. Once packaged, the price goes up to somewhere between 5 cents and 25 cents per cup, depending on the brand.

The price jumps again, to $1 or a $1.50 per cup, as it moves into the diner or the local restaurant. This increase occurs because the product, coffee, has now been wrapped in a service. A waitress or counter worker has to brew it and serve it to you in a nice clean white mug. And as companies started creating just the right experience and ambiance, the price elevates to $2 or even $5 per cup.

At this point, consumers are paying for much more than coffee. They are paying for the experience of purchasing and consuming the coffee.

Today, coffee can be purchased at many places, all of which offer very different experiences. The consumers who purchase the coffee from these different places are doing so to *feel* something, to tap into who they are or who they aspire to be.

Because the commodity is a critical part of that experience, it becomes something more to the consumer: it is part of the consumer's life, either as a status symbol, a comfort, or even a stance. Those who choose not to buy their coffee from Starbucks are making just as significant a statement about who they are and what they believe as the people that prefer the *Starbucks experience*.

And as important as this encounter is to consumers, it is even more important to Starbucks. The company has designed it to work in a certain way. For instance, Starbucks knows that being hit with the smell of coffee upon walking into one of its shops is crucial to its patrons. So when the company decided to add hot food to the menu, it commissioned the creation of an oven that would not allow any of the food smells to seep into the store environment. Starbucks didn't want anything to affect that coffee smell its patrons enjoy when they visit and spend time enjoying the *Starbucks experience*.

Compare that to Dunkin' Donuts, a brand whose coffee is actually secondary to its main product. Dunkin' Donuts has much more limited coffee selections, and many of its stores don't encourage the hang out model of Starbucks. The prevalent smell in its stores is the baked goods.

Neither experience is right or wrong. However, various consumers' decisions to participate in one or the other is really a desire to say something about themselves. Starbucks knows this and makes sure nothing affects the primary tenets that are attributed to its brand experience.

To give you a little preview of what's to come in this book regarding laddering, I'll add a personal element to this example. As I shared in the book's Preface, I love to travel. I also love Starbucks. Anyone who visits my office will see both of my passions on display. I have Starbucks city mugs from the many places I have visited covering my office. By doing so, I am exhibiting something to those visiting me that's much more than a simple mug collection. I have associated myself with a certain caché to the Starbucks brand and am also expressing that I am well traveled. These mugs go beyond just a collection and tell people something about how I see myself.

The example of coffee is one of my favorites to explain how the world has changed. My business partner at User Insight had basically the same demographic characteristics as me: same gender and roughly the same age, income level, and location. But he is a Dunkin' Donuts guy, whereas I prefer Starbucks. If someone were to view us solely through the lens of demographics, they would completely miss the mark about how to market to us as individuals.

Now you may read this section and think to yourself, "I could care less about the experience of coffee." But chances are that there's something else that *is* important, some other way you choose to express yourself. Context is crucial to understanding and uncovering the lessons that laddering offers and to truly map your consumers' DNA.

Technology advances such as the personal computer, the Internet, and further advances in the ability to support mass production at higher and higher levels through globalization required companies to do something more than just offer a product. Although the experience economy was part of the answer, it was still bound by some of the old rules and was predictably measured by standard practices. After all, the Internet is really just another mass media channel, especially when the technology is expensive and the available bandwidth is limited.

The experience economy was merely the tip of the iceberg for what we are currently experiencing in the space of consumer selection and knowledge. The Internet helped support and added some level of complexity to this trend. But more than that, it actually reinforced the long-held belief that looking at what people were doing and buying could help us figure out how to affect sales, marketing, and the bottom line.

We learned that if we change the online message slightly, or even the price, we can watch sales grow. Companies ran split tests on messages and interactions; within hours, they were able to determine whether a change had negatively or positively affected their bottom line. They could have actually gained more control over how consumers entered their channels and viewed their products.

Many of the projects we signed at User Insight came from such insights and knowledge. We received frantic calls from researchers or product managers, wondering how their best performing online property was off by one or two basis points because of slight changes in the experience. We would shepherd the product through the lab, determine the root cause, and then create a course of action to remedy the problem.

The history I have shared in this chapter spans almost 100 years. The world of mass production and mass media stood true for that extended period. Marketers and product developers could rely on known facts and constants that were established during this era to determine the way forward.

Those were the "good old days" of a mere five years ago, before the world changed forever to one where consumers are highly informed and definitely in charge. Consumers today have an almost unlimited number of choices, a voice to express their frustrations and their delights, and a tendency to rely on other consumers to confirm their choices. They do not base their decisions on a brand's marketing or a salesperson's advice.

In this world, *what* they do is far less important than *why* they do it. And we cannot develop an understanding of *who* they are solely by looking at what's on the surface. In this new world, marketing and product development need to understand the consumer better than the consumer understands himself or herself. And the following chapters will tell you how to do just that.

> ## Key Points
>
> - Mass production was initially invented to support the war effort; however, it posed a problem because consistent demand is needed to support mass production.
> - Consumerism was then developed to solve the problem that mass production posed. Its goal was to incite need, which was aimed to make consumers want goods, services, and products that were previously available only to very few as a luxury.
> - Limited information and few channels (mass media) allowed marketers to control the message that consumers received. Marketers used this control to convince people to buy and to influence and shape the public's perception of brands, products, and companies.
> - Consumerism was further enhanced as a result of increased affluence and people's desire to fit in.
> - Although the Internet promised a deeper understanding of the individual, it and the experience economy were based on a mass media model and served to reinforce the notion of consumers as groups that could be marketed to as a group, not understood as individuals.
> - Today's technology and the ability to mass customize products have changed this environment forever. Consumers now want and expect to be understood as individuals.

---

[2] Larry Tye, *Father of Spin: Edward L. Bernays and the Birth of PR* (New York: Picador, 2002), 18–19.

2

The Need for Laddering

Toto, I have a feeling we're not in Kansas anymore.
—Dorothy, The Wizard of Oz

I'VE ALWAYS BEEN a great swimmer and feel at home in any kind of water: beach, lake, pool, or river—you name it. My dream is to live by the water and walk on the beach every day, and my favorite form of exercise is swimming laps at a local pool.

I was, apparently, a fan of the water my entire life. My parents tell stories of me as a toddler running toward the pool and jumping in at full force, unaware—due to my lack of experience—of the dangers that existed. I went on to become a very good swimmer and spent my elementary years at the pool and participated in our neighborhood's swim team.

However, I can distinctly remember one instance where the water became a new and frightening environment for me, different from the familiar one I'd come to know. I was nine years old, visiting a local water park and playing in one of those huge wave pools. With each crashing wave, an undertow pulled me farther and farther out to a sudden drop-off in the pool that put the water well over my head. I was out of my mother's reach and in serious trouble. Luckily, she quickly realized I was in trouble and jumped into action. She had the strength to pull me back to safety, but not before I took several gulps of water and saw my short life flash before my eyes.

This is what has happened in the world of product development and marketing in the past few years. The calm, predictable waters—that is, the formulas that have worked for decades to predict sales and adoption—are no longer enough to be successful. As a result, today's marketing and product development managers find themselves in the same predicament as was I in that wave pool: they are in over their head, being pulled farther out and being asked to support more and more technology. They need to create products that still appeal to a wide group of people while analyzing a growing

21

mountain of data. They are looking for a lifeline, a way to get their head above water, find their footing, and understand the new way forward.

The initial cracks in the old way of building and distributing products came with the introduction of the iPod in October 2001. Even though it was a mass-produced item, it disrupted a single industry by fundamentally changing the way we bought, consumed, and shared music. Yet what some people don't know is that Apple wasn't the first company with an MP3 player on the market. SaeHan, an electronics device company, was selling one in Asia called MPMan as early as the spring of 1998.

What Apple did that SaeHan missed was make it easy for users to include this product in their lives in the way the consumer saw fit. And soon enough, we were hooked on this new gadget, with very little overt direction from the product creator on how to use it. The technology for accomplishing this was truly as simple as plug and play, and instead of selling it to us based on gigabytes or RAM or through any other technical jargon, Apple simply let us know that as a user, you could have "1,000 songs in your pocket." The iPod's advertisement emphasized the joy of listening untethered to our own music through iconic white earphones. None of these advertisements included the technical jargon usually associated with a technology product. They simply showed a darkened shadow dancing to music; the only words that ever appeared were *iPod* or *iPod + iTunes*.

Before the iPod came along, recording artists carefully compiled their playlists. But this new device did something seemingly revolutionary: by providing iTunes, an easy-to-use software product, it allowed us to create our own playlists based on our desires or mood, thereby allowing us to craft our own experience. As a result, many of us may never buy an entire album again—and we certainly wouldn't listen to it in the way that had been dictated by the artist in the past.

Then Apple upped the odds even further with subsequent versions of the iPod, adding video, increasing storage, and decreasing its footprint. Soon, this vehicle of experience and customization became virtually everyone's must-have item.

But the crashing waves didn't really hit until June 29, 2007. That was the date when Apple introduced a product that—in a very short timeframe—*fundamentally* changed the way we could customize devices that we carry with us everywhere: the iPhone.

Before this point, every phone that was manufactured had to contain common elements: buttons, placement of icons, and even applications. There was no way to customize the experience at the base level in the way that the iPhone and other smartphones eventually accomplished.

Back then, a lot of phones looked the same. But today, if you took a picture of the main page of everyone's smartphone, you'd find that no two were alike. If you looked closer and began to determine the types of apps that were on each, you would be able to identify patterns by analyzing what individuals are including on their phones. No two smartphones contain the same apps, and even if they did, there's a good chance those apps are not being used in the same way or for the same primary purpose.

The introduction of smartphones combined with countless apps, social media, e-books, a fundamentally changed economy, and a constantly maturing, ever-present Internet have provided us with the ability to access information and data anywhere, anytime. It's no wonder we have been left gulping for air with little understanding as to what just happened.

The world has changed—*dramatically*.

And thanks to these changes, companies that have traditionally developed and marketed products and services based on market segmentation and demographics are floundering. Their assumptions that their products' features, functionalities, and messaging will meet all consumers' needs in a given demographic—a one size fits all mentality—no longer works.

Some companies continue to believe that they will magically be able to go back to the good old days by mining their big data to look for patterns. They believe they can return to a time when it was enough to simply add their system-collected knowledge to what they gathered from census data or transactions, and then use the results to peg and speak to their end consumers. Back then, companies needed to know only that a person was at certain life stage or had a certain purchase history in order to reach him or her and be successful. That no longer gets the job done.

In today's many-to-many world, users group themselves largely based on values, interests, and aspirations, not according to traditional segmentations of sex, race, and age. You must understand these consumers at their core, that is, what drives them and how they act (and want to act) within certain contexts. You will learn as we talk about this new approach that consumers are far more driven by their desire to share, their desire for authenticity, and their need for relationships. And although this new consumer mind-set was unleashed by advances in technology, it goes beyond technology-based products, solutions, and experiences.

Companies must also realize that they can no longer rely on reaching consumers through mass media channels or influencing via testimonials, celebrity endorsements, or other traditional tried-and-true ways to promote and sell products and services. Much of what affects people's buying decisions today is invisible and unseen; it's private and something that only the specific consumer knows. Today's drivers can be as simple as getting a recommendation from a blog or a tweet from an author upon whom the consumer relies—because they feel like they are alike. It can be a desire to stay connected in the physical world with those they love and care about. It may even be in pursuit of satisfying some deeper need of understanding or acceptance that they carry with them and seek to satisfy by the way they relate to the world around them.

The Answer: Laddering Your Consumer

Technology is no longer the complicated part of the equation; today, it is a given—even easy. Much of the technology currently available is almost as easy and intuitive for us to use as a doorknob or a pencil. There are proven, known ways to make the technology work, so focusing on best practices here would be somewhat of a fool's errand.

The fact is that humans are *good* at picking up and using new tools. We adopt them into our environment and start using them to accomplish the task at hand. But because this comes so effortlessly to us, we tend to ignore the larger impact the tool may have on us. And if it's hard to recognize these changes in ourselves, it's even harder to discern them and their impact in others. That's why this most recent disruption's effects on us have been so difficult to recognize and sort out.

Think about how you would survive a day at the mall without your cell phone. From making a simple phone call, to finding the store that has what you need, to texting back and forth regarding meeting up with friends, and to ensure no one is duplicating a birthday gift purchase. Consumers of all stages of demographics quickly and effortlessly include the cell phone and its many facets of utility into their lives—and can't imagine what life was like before them.

We must therefore start focusing on what's complicated: us, the consumer, the user. The adage "Know thy user" has never been more important than it is now—and will be ever more important in coming years.

Companies must now understand their users' behaviors and core motivators—that is, know the *whys* behind consumers' actions.

Only after understanding this and figuring out how to insert themselves into the consumers' existing buying journey will companies be able to establish what consumers really want, which, in most cases, is a relationship. In a relationship, the company understands when to deliver the right message to the right person at the right time and across the right channel. The company can anticipate the consumer's needs and add the appropriate functionality, features, and experience to their products and services.

Today's connected consumers demand more from companies than a reliance on demographics, segmentation, or other big data will reveal. They have very specific expectations of brands to provide them with a product, service, or experience. The recent dramatic disruptions in the buyer journey means that companies can no longer rely on previously proven models of reaching their consumer audience or expect these consumers to follow the traditional path from identifying a need to making a purchase.

As I see marketing venture into collecting more and more data on those they are selling to, I notice that they're just like I was as a nine-year-old in a wave pool: they are jumping into something and not fully sure of what they are getting into. Many expect that they will somehow be able to unlock what everything means and discover how to react once they have determined the data's patterns.

But this isn't how it works. Some of these patterns no longer matter, whereas some others mean virtually everything. As this land grab for big data continues, the companies that can unlock the *important* patterns through the filter of the consumer will be the winners.

The purpose of this book is to do just that: to discuss the patterns of consumer behavior that are truly important—what I call *consumer DNA*—and to understand how to determine your own consumer's unique DNA and capitalize on it for successful products, service, experiences, and marketing messages.

In the upcoming chapters, I will discuss the specific steps you can take to start laddering your consumers to understand them. Before we discuss the specific steps and the process, I will cover important aspects of laddering.

Laddering Is Continual Learning

Most companies I work with tend to ask at the beginning of every laddering engagement, "How long is this going to take? When will you know something?"

My answer is always, "I will know what I know when I know it."

It's a lot like the concept of balance; no one can explain it. You can't see it; you just know it after you've achieved it through practice. You have to think about the concept of laddering the same way. You don't know what you have until you have it.

Of course, there are some rules of thumb and proven approaches to laddering your consumers. You must keep in mind that it's about getting beneath the core drivers and motivations to understand *why* consumers behave the way they do. What are they trying to express or accomplish? What do they *really* want?

Answering these questions requires a fairly broad approach—one that strives to truly understand the consumers you want to reach. There needs to be an understanding relationship between people, brands, and products in order to thrive in today's economy. Although many people claim that this kind of relationship was destroyed by the Internet and associated technologies, it is actually more important today than it's ever been before. The difference is simply that the Internet, and in particular social media, has changed the way we form, foster, and rely upon these relationships in a very powerful way. We connect with people based on common interests and beliefs, and others' influence on us is strongly based on how much those people care and foster their bonds with us.

Laddering Uncovers Relationship

We see this desire for relationship and understanding in the ways people use technology and social media. It's never been easier to connect with other people in general; specifically, our ability to discover and interact with those with whom we share common interests is supported in newer, more interesting ways every day.

Consider the website Pinterest, which was introduced in closed beta in March 2010 and is used largely for the visual collection of images—images of ideas, aspirations, inspiration, and achievements. The segmentation here isn't based on age, gender, or location, but rather on what people like to spend their time doing, seeing, eating, and so forth. So many people have used their boards to share ideas for their upcoming nuptials that there is a start-up company taking the Pinterest idea a step further by creating a "Pinterest for Weddings."

Google+ is another technology that's touted as a backbone for the Internet, helping people find connections to others with similar interests, thereby making everyone's recommendations more appropriate and useful. Because so many of us have learned to group people based on demographic characteristics, segmentation, and lifestyle, I was guilty of this myself when I first set up Google+. I used categories such as:

- Atlanta
- Entrepreneurs
- User Insight
- User experience

For Google+ to be most effective, I should really sort my circle more like this:

- Foodies (people who like restaurants and food similar to my taste)

- Music (people who share my taste in music and concerts)
- Travel (people who share my interests in travel locations and experiences)

By using this approach, I get much better recommendations in my Google results. Organizing people based on segmentation or demographic data is not as helpful, because I only care to receive suggestions from people who I know are like me within certain contexts—and my age, location, and job aren't often important. For instance, I'd much rather get a recommendation for restaurants or food experiences from a fellow foodie versus a fellow entrepreneur.

This is a simple example of how an individual can use laddering. Once you are in relationship with others, you automatically start to sort their recommendations and follow their actions based on how closely you think they map to your own personal beliefs, preferences, and points of view. It's something you do subconsciously, because it's how you learn to survive and thrive in your environment.

For marketing and product development to get it right as they move forward, they need to understand where their product and/ or brand fits in relation to consumers who *naturally* associate themselves with the brand. Companies cannot force their goods on an end consumer; rather, consumers carefully choose what they want to include in their lives in the same way they choose the friends they hang out with.

Executing laddering properly takes a methodical effort. Once you figure it out, you can rely on the results for many years to come.

I'm frequently perplexed by the approach that some companies take. There are so many that don't think twice about spending the money and effort required to build a safe, reliable product yet hesitate to take the time and effort to make sure they are building products the end consumer *really wants*. I have the same opinion about the number of dollars that exchange hands in the advertising and marketing space solely based on demographics and Nielsen ratings. This disregard for knowing the end consumer is the result of so many companies' inability to understand and react according to today's changed environment, particularly in the marketing and product development space.

Laddering Is Long Lasting

How long will this work last? I always get this question at the end of a presentation or a specific laddering exercise.

The great thing about laddering is that it's based on an individual's core, something that rarely, if ever, changes. If it does, it takes a dramatic disruption. Often, marketers confuse the concept of a person's core with life stage because life stages often come with a change in the fundamental way that a cluster (distinct consumer groups that map to one another because of their core DNA or behavior) approaches a problem.

For example, a newly married couple may change their spending habits because one of them is a saver and the other is the spender. If the couple chooses to save, the spender in the marriage will begin to manifest spending in a different way. We have seen spenders use coupons and point collection or rewards programs to support their underlying desire to continue to spend. None of these activities are actually *saving*, though; they are just special ways of spending. Savers never spend their money; they get their satisfaction from watching their money grow. No matter how good the coupon or the deal is, savers will find a reason to delay the purchase. Marriage and other life stages do not change their core.

Laddering Establishes a Common Language

Consider the topic of banking. Most banks' messaging has focused on life stage drivers. Newly married? Saving for retirement? Time for college?

However, we gathered some interesting information in our laddering work in the space of financial services, specifically as it relates to choice or acquisition of a bank. As it happens, the drivers behind this choice fall into three large categories that have *nothing* to do with one's life stage.

To get to these three categories, we had to dig underneath a word that kept coming up over and over again in our conversations with consumers: *convenience.* Everyone told us that they choose a bank or financial institution based on this word, but *convenience* means something different to different people. If we had followed the standard quantification and segmentation studies surrounding bank choice as being driven by a life stage, we likely would have identified the word *convenience,* but we would have risked recommending messaging similar to this:

- ABC Bank has the most convenient process for consolidating your bank accounts after marriage.
- ABC Bank makes it convenient for you to plan for your retirement.
- The most convenient college savings accounts are found at ABC Bank.

But this wasn't the answer. *Convenience* means something different to three distinct groups, and it doesn't matter if you are a baby boomer or a Gen Yer; bank choice is based on one of the following drivers: locations and branches, online tools, or personal relationship.

- *Locations and Branches:* Consumers who define convenience as locations and branches are family-centered and spend a lot of time with relatives and in their community. They are constantly on the go, heading to school, sports events, and church activities. To them, banks are a physical space, and it's important to have convenient access near both home and work. They like that the tellers recognize them when they are at the bank and enjoy the person-to-person interaction when they are making a transaction. They don't see banks as the place for "important" financial matters. They prefer to handle such things themselves or use a secondary brokerage firm or financial planner. A move to a new town might mean a change in banking relationship if their current bank doesn't have physical bank locations (ATMs, branches) readily available.

- *Online Tools:* Consumers who define convenience based on online tools will describe their lives as busy with friends, family, and work. The Internet and other task-specific apps are great tools for helping them stay organized, efficient, and informed. They research everything online and are savvy, efficient online shoppers. They spend time reading reviews and comparing options before making a final choice. They love their bank or financial institution because of the tools they provide, but they rarely, if ever, actually visit a branch. In fact, they are more likely than the other two groups to use a bank that doesn't even have nearby physical branch locations or ATMs. The uncoupling cost to this group for switching banks is high, because they have invested so much time and process in existing online tools such as bill pay. They are open to push messages regarding new products and services if those messages are specifically tailored to their needs. After all, their bank knows a lot about them. They feel that the bank should therefore use this information to enhance their messages' relevance, ultimately saving this group time.

- *Personal Relationship:* Convenience for third group is determined by personal relationships. They have a more complex financial picture, perhaps from receiving an inheritance, starting a small business, or achieving other financial success, and time is truly a finite commodity. They spend time online but not on research or comparison activities. They have a network of trusted advisors who help point them to others who will meet their needs and provide the high-touch personal relationship they desire. They expect to be able to call or e-mail a specific individual within the bank to take care of their needs, and this person should already know their unique situation without explanation. They will switch banks only for a better relationship. The consumers would enter the banking choice in three different ways as illustrated in Figure 2.1.

It's crucial to define broad, everyday terms such as *convenience* according to what the consumer or end user really means. It's easy to take common words and assume a definition. But understanding *why* a person uses that word—and what value it has to his or her core needs—is the real solution to building messages and products that resonate with your consumer groups.

Figure 2.1 *Convenience* **is the Core Driver Behind Bank Choice**

These consumer groups' core preferences are not likely to change; therefore, the laddering results will apply for a long time to come. The only reason to do another laddering project would be if another disruption hits the space. For example, the growth of the Internet in the mid-1990s created one of these groups—the group that equates convenience to online tools. Of course, disruptions can be factors beyond technology. This project was completed at the same time that the economic meltdown occurred. We had to account for the disruption around banking and trust of banks. It would also make sense to revisit the research to see if social media or mobile apps have had any impact on how these groups define and expect relationship with their banks today across these new mediums. The base knowledge provides a great starting point to build upon and test some hypotheses.

Laddering Uncovers Influence

One of the traps I often see companies fall into when starting a laddering project is to focus on the *size* of the groups (clusters). Although the question of size is important, it's not as crucial as it was in the days of quantification and segmentation. What's much more important now is an understanding of *influence*.

We have worked on projects where the size of a group was too small to be considered significant for a brand based on the rules of quantification and segmentation. However, if we had ignored the group, the product or campaign would have been a complete failure. It's therefore crucial to understand the following as you undergo the laddering exercise:

1. *The influence of a cluster:* Do others listen and care when this group says something?
2. *The ecosystem of the cluster:* To whom are they naturally attached, and where do they get their information?

An understanding of this relationship—and the connection to your product or brand that flows from it—is far more important than any number can express. There are countless examples today of how influential just *one person* can be, especially given our ability to easily broadcast our messages far and wide.

I recently attended a panel on Pinterest at Digital Atlanta, an annual conference in Atlanta, that highlighted how powerful a single person can really be in our new highly connected society. Kirsten Kowalski was a participant on the panel about Pinterest and shared the following experience:

Kirsten is a photographer *and* a lawyer who decided to read through the image use policy of Pinterest. After doing so, she penned the blog post "Why I Tearfully Deleted My Pinterest Inspiration Boards," posted it, and then went to bed. She awoke the next morning to find that her website was no longer working. Assuming that it was merely a technology glitch, she called her web host provider, who informed her that she had surpassed the allowed traffic to her site overnight.

Kirsten's blog post had gone viral. She had more than 700 responses from others across the web regarding her decision. She even received a call from Pinterest founder Ben Silbermann to discuss her concerns. The site probably didn't expect one person's words to influence the Pinterest ecosystem so significantly. By spending time early on to understand Kirsten and others like her, Pinterest may have been able to craft language that was more palatable to people who held the same core drivers—mainly, a desire to do what was right. The good news is that Pinterest reacted quickly and correctly to the post and participated actively in the resolution.

Before undergoing the exercise of laddering your consumers and putting them into their discrete groups, you must rethink everything you have considered about large quantification studies and work to understand and anticipate the new power and reach of the individual.

The Need for Laddering the Consumer

Important changes have taken place in our world that impact the way we interact, both with it and with one another. These changes call for innovative methods to function and operate, especially when it comes to creating new products, services, experiences, and marketing messages. In the next chapter, I will cover the concept of laddering, how it's been used in the past to sell what could be produced, and how it can be used to understand what's most important now: the consumer.

Key Points

- The introduction of disruptive technology such as smartphones and social media has forever changed the consumer landscape by allowing consumers more choice and individual customization.
- Relying on group size to predict consumer behavior is an outdated and dangerous approach; it leads brands to create products and services based on drivers that are not important to their consumers.
- Consumers sort themselves into self-selected groups based on a variety of factors, such as specific interests. These interests could include types of restaurants or experiences they enjoy. They do not conform to being sorted according to the traditional demographic divisions.
- Using a common language when talking with your consumers ensures greater success and understanding of what products to build and marketing messages to launch.
- Laddering is a continual learning process that helps you establish relationships with your consumers in a new way.
- The individual has more power to influence than in any other period in modern history, and the time to start laddering your consumers for greater understanding is now.

BellSouth Case Study: But Would You?

User Insight's first application of laddering consumers to unlock their unique DNA happened in 2004. We initially used this approach in our work with BellSouth, a local provider of Internet service that AT&T eventually purchased.

We had worked with BellSouth for years and had completed extensive work with their customer support teams. The primary goals of our partnership were to (1) reduce the number of phone calls and (2) get customers to install DSL on their own without a technician's help. In other words, BellSouth wanted to change its consumers' behavior by making them more self-sufficient.

BellSouth was very loyal about bringing products into our lab, because its overall objective was to allow end consumers to diagnose support problems for themselves. Throughout its history as a company, BellSouth had strongly believed in putting products in front of its customers as a means to test messaging, features, and acceptance. The company also wanted to cut down on its support costs; at that time, it cost the company $17 per call just to answer the call, an amount that didn't even include the costs involved in actually taking the time to diagnose the customer's problem.

We were conducting the research while BellSouth was attempting to convert as many customers as possible from dial-up to DSL. Although this conversion initially seemed like a great idea, it only compounded the potential burden on the company's support desk, since nontechnical people were expected to navigate what was a relatively new and technically complicated product.

(continued)

(continued)

We had worked with BellSouth's primary desktop product, called FastAccess Help Center, through many iterations. The product was automatically installed as part of the DSL installation CD; its purpose was to serve as a desktop guide for installing and diagnosing problems with DSL service.

After developing several versions of the product and conducting studies through our lab, BellSouth created one that successfully got lab respondents to reconnect a loose wire or diagnose problems with settings that had been changed on their machine. The problem, of course, is that our lab is an artificial setting. We were giving these respondents tasks, and even though we weren't directing them to do so, they were following steps and playing along because they were in a lab setting and had received a scenario to follow. Frankly, they would do anything we asked as long as they got their promised $100 at the end of the session. There was no way to tell if the effects would translate as seamlessly to a real-life situation.

The problem was that we never asked respondents, "Would you use this application instead of picking up the phone?" That is, if you were in your own home—not in a lab where you are being paid to perform—would you diagnose these problems and follow through on your own? Would you even think to open this application and actually do what it is telling you to do?

We attempted to answer that question by undertaking a large project. In it, we aimed to spend time in people's homes, watching them struggle with the same problems they had been presented with in our lab, but in an environment that

Figure 2.2 Customers Clustered around the Motivations of *Need to Be Connected* and *Willingness to Troubleshoot*

(we hoped) would provide much more honest and realistic answers to our questions. As a result, we made some rich discoveries about the true motivations, drivers, and propensity of these people to undertake this level of self-support, all of which are depicted in Figure 2.2.

The factors that were important in this study to the clusters were the need to be connected to the Internet and their willingness to troubleshoot on their own.

We assign names to the clusters to make them more real. It provides an easy way to reference the cluster when talking

(continued)

(continued)

with others, both team members and those new to the findings. It's also more natural to remember the cluster by a name than by a behavior. By giving them an easy-to-remember name, the clusters become part of your team, just like they are sitting in a meeting next to you.

Our most technically competent cluster, Milton, whom you see at the top right, would never install the FastAccess Help Center product. He saw it as a resource hog and thought he knew more than what it or any support representative, for that matter, would suggest. He had a high need to be connected to the Internet and would work through any channel necessary to get his connection back up and running.

On the other side of the spectrum is our least technical cluster, Arthur, who could go days without Internet access and not be bothered. We even joked that you had to call Arthur to tell him that someone had sent him an e-mail. Members of this group saw Internet access as a luxury, not a necessity. They were willing to pay either in time or money to have someone fix the problem for them.

Cindy was the "path of least resistance" cluster. Although she needed to be connected, she didn't want to be bothered with having to understand how to correct problems with the connection. She would call her neighbor or rope a coworker into fixing it for her. Cindy didn't have time to spend on the phone with a support rep, nor did she have the desire to be "taught" why it wasn't working. It didn't fit in her realm of understanding, and she didn't see how learning it would help her in the future.

We found in this study, and every BellSouth study after, that we could ask three simple behavioral questions to pinpoint a respondent's cluster type. In fact, we conducted one study recently in the area of parenting styles that required us to ask only a single question to discern whether we were providing the right content and message to the right person The questions for BellSouth included prompts such as "Do you go to the store to buy technology on your own (Milton), or take someone with you (Cindy)?" All of our questions were forced choice and meant to understand a consumers' core behavior.

After completing the in-context work, we spent time on the phone with the representatives manning the support desks. We learned during that phase of the research, much to our dismay, many of the support personnel were advising the customer to uninstall the FastAccess Help Center product altogether! This advice certainly defeated the intended purpose of the product in reducing support costs because, after all, if the product wasn't available to the customer, it would be impossible for it to help that person with support issues.

This stresses a point that's crucial to every laddering effort: to truly resolve an issue, you must not only hit your goals with a sales and marketing campaign but also look at a problem from every part of your organization. It's not enough to fix a product if the group supporting or promoting the product doesn't know the intended purpose—or worse, does something that counteracts your efforts.

The other cool thing is that we could start to peg which cluster the caller belonged to by the way that person worded his or her questions and whether the support representative's advice was heeded or ignored. The more trusting and naive the consumer was (Arthur and Tina, for example), the more likely he or she was to follow the advice. The more technically apt ones (Milton) were less likely to follow advice.

(continued)

(continued)

One truly fantastic aspect of this project was that we were able to supplement it by recruiting a panel of customers to move from dial-up to DSL. We enlisted an equal distribution of the clusters identified during the laddering exercise and gave them incentive to upgrade to DSL. Because we knew the clusters so well, we could predict which groups were going to respond to which of our surveys, even before we served them the next exercise or task to complete. We always had to prompt the less involved group (Cindy) to respond to our inquiries, whereas the more technical group provided us with more detail than we ever cared to review.

One of the most significant takeaways from this project was BellSouth's acceptance that it couldn't *force* certain clusters to change their behavior. And because the customer wouldn't adapt, that meant the company had to.

Solving support problems served as a precursor to our current many-to-many relational environment, because it requires a similar interaction to that which we see in social media and is supported by the latest disruptive technologies. Providing support is and always will be relational. To properly support someone else in a situation, you must come to an understanding of the issues—specifically, *why* there is an issue and how it affects the consumer.

Our work with BellSouth prompted the company to look at its customers in a new way. It highlighted opportunities that went far beyond just correcting a single support application. This foundational research directed our way forward on future work with BellSouth. In addition, we were able to use the knowledge we gathered across many of their other subsequent projects and product rollouts. We could predict which consumer clusters would react positively or negatively to new support approaches or ideas just by understanding where they fell in the clusters developed.

The revelations of this project were in part what caused our focus as an organization to change. Although we had always cared about and advocated for the user, we had also always focused on changes in technology best practice. In essence, our goal had been to simplify a process to fewer steps or move an element up or down on a page. But this project opened our eyes to how important it was to start looking at these core consumer drivers as often as our projects allowed. Just like my first experience in a usability lab, this change in organizational focus came at the perfect time for a marketplace and environment on the verge of dramatic transformation.

3

Laddering Defined

A lot of people in our industry haven't had very diverse experiences. So they don't have enough dots to connect, and they end up with very linear solutions without a broad perspective on the problem. The broader one's understanding of the human experience, the better design we will have.
—Steve Jobs

LIKE MANY PEOPLE, one of my passions is cooking. I love to spend a Sunday afternoon tackling a complex recipe, and my favorites are those you find in magazines such as *Cook's Illustrated*. This is because I know that the writers and editors at *Cook's Illustrated* have spent countless hours trying every conceivable combination of a recipe to come up with one that works just right. The standard, "proven" techniques that other recipes or cooks advocate are often disproved in the *Cook's Illustrated* kitchen. This publication and the people who work for it often take a counterintuitive approach to common thinking. Some of my best, and simplest, recipes come from understanding how they have approached the science of cooking differently—the fact that they have taken a broader stroke and determined how to approach individual components of the entire meal, instead of focusing only on the end goal.

The same is true in regard to the concept of laddering. This approach advocates that we take a different approach than the ones we've followed before to truly succeed in the space of marketing and product development.

Before I begin my discussion about laddering's application in detail, I think it's important to know how this technique has been discussed previously.

The concept of laddering was originally developed during a time that all products were mass-produced. Prior work in the area of laddering concentrated on what features and functions a product had. We then moved the user out from that "feature, function" list to determine what was most important to the consumer when making the decision to buy the product—and to determine what messages or approach brands should use to sell the product to the consumer.

Remember that mass production assumes that you are building a product—a clock radio, watch, toy, or phone, for example—for

47

the masses as cheaply as possible. Therefore, an item's features and functions are very important in this environment, because they're really the only things that distinguish one product or service from another. So to decide whether a consumer would buy or not, it was important to ask, "Are the features and functions the right ones for that specific individual?" The earlier concept of laddering focused on creating the right messaging, not necessarily the right product. The message had to be compelling to make the product as enticing as possible.

Thomas J. Reynolds, a consumer researcher and professor, and Jonathan Gutman, a marketer and professor, developed and introduced laddering in 1988, based on Gutman's Means-End Theory of 1982. Their approach states that product *attributes* lead to *consequences* that generate *personal meaning (values)* for users. In other words, they worked from the starting point of features to determine which functional and emotional benefits resonate with the consumer.

Consumers who were presented with a set of features and benefits prior to mass customization would opt for the product that best satisfied their emotions and beliefs. They would rationalize the purchase by focusing on the features and functional benefits. These consumers didn't have the number of choices or the amount of knowledge we have when making a buying decision today.

The process involved in this type of laddering work went something like this:

First, the marketer would ask: *"Which feature do you like best about this product?"*

The marketer would listen to the answer and then ask about functional benefit. *"What does the feature do?"*

After getting this response, the marketer would then ask about the *higher* benefit of the functional benefit; that is, *"How does that feature benefit you?"*

Finally, the marketer would ask about the higher benefit's emotional benefit: *"How does the feature benefit make you feel?"*

Once a feature had been exhausted, marketers would ask the consumer about his or her next favorite feature and its functional, higher, and emotional benefits. The order in which these elements are listed became the hierarchy by which the brand promoted it to the consumer.

To put this into context, think about purchasing a stereo system for your home. A consumer buying this kind of item would consider the features and put them in order of priority. After doing so, the consumer would determine which feature was most important to him or her. In this example, we will assume the CD changer is the highest-valued feature of the stereo system:

Question	Answer
What feature do you like best?	I like the CD changer.
What does the feature do?	It allows me to play multiple CDs.
How does the feature benefit you?	It means that I don't have to constantly change out CDs.
What does the benefit do for you?	The CDs can just play in the background while I cook dinner or host a party.

The process is then repeated for the rest of the stereo system's features and functions based on the consumer's priority until all are exhausted.

This approach *was* appropriate once upon a time, when it was crucial to start the process by focusing on features or functions and understanding their place of priority. Sellers essentially said: "I start with what I can do for consumers, what can I mass-produce to meet their needs, and understand what their higher-order needs are in order to sell them the product."

This worked well for Edward Bernays's work (see Chapter 1), specifically, to understand how to make a consumer want what vendors could make. And because the seller also controlled the message, advertisers could create this sense of wanting by understanding how to speak to consumers' higher-order desires. *"Want to be cool at your next party? Our stereo system lets you concentrate on your friends and entertaining them while the music you select plays in the background."*

Laddering in a User-Centered World

However, we've now moved from a world of mass production to one of mass *customization*. Our current environment has made the consumer the complicated part of the equation. It's therefore crucial to understand them and what they want, because their selection of features and functions are numerous—and require very low switching costs.

This is a good opportunity to discuss two fairly well-known quotes about the value of qualitative research techniques such as laddering that are actually misunderstood.

The first comes from Henry Ford, who is credited as having said the following about the creation of the automobile: "If I had asked people what they wanted, they would have said faster horses."

The other is attributed to Steve Jobs about the invention of new products, and it basically says the same thing in a simpler way: "People can't tell you what they want."

Although it's true that both of these statements were uttered by the men noted, their meaning has been somewhat twisted and misinterpreted over the years. I often see these quotes on the signature lines of marketers, designers, or product managers as justification for creating in a vacuum using only their own instincts.

What Henry Ford and Steve Jobs were saying is that the average person doesn't know how to *build* a product. This is true, and I agree with both of them on that point. That's why we have product designers.

We can find good analogy for understanding what you *should* do in the profession of architecture. When you commission an architect to design a house for you, you tell him or her what you want and then trust that professional to interpret your desires into the drawings of the house. Good architects would meet you in your current space and have you walk through what you like, what you would change, and how you want to use the space differently. From this context, they can interpret what to recommend to you in a new space.

Once the architect creates the plans, he or she would walk you through the newly conceived space. At that point, you can provide a solid reaction to what you like or don't like about how the plan has been laid out.

What Steve Jobs and Henry Ford were saying is that product designers and marketers must become architects of what consumers want to buy and how they already perceive brands or products. As it was with cars and iPods, consumers may not be able to tell you what to build or precisely *how* to design a product. However, they can certainly express met and unmet needs (the need to go faster or to have their music more conveniently accessible, for instance). And as both Ford and Jobs knew, the future in product development and innovation will always be in understanding where these unmet needs lead—the white space between the consumer and what technology, products, or services currently do or do not do for them.

To start addressing these unmet needs, you must understand your end consumers on a base level. The only way to do this is to get in front of them and engage them in discussions in the context or environment where they will use your product or consider your brand.

Laddering Understands the Consumer's Context

We all put on masks and present ourselves in a certain way when we go out into public. But if you opened the drawers in our houses, looked in our pockets, or examined our closets, you would find a very different person—with very different motivation.

This is why I interview people one on one, where they live, work, and play, whenever possible. I "go native" with the consumer to truly understand who that person is and how he or she lives. I have been around the world to spend time with end users in manufacturing plants, grain elevators, high-rise apartments, trailer parks, dairy farms, country clubs, and everywhere in between to make certain I could really get to the core of what a user was telling me.

By getting into the consumers' space, I can go beyond the needs that they express overtly through spoken words. It's actually rare that a consumer will say, "I really wish this product would do *this*." The best and most effective way to understand your consumers is to experience them in their own environments and using their own technology or devices to survive and navigate their own worlds.

When you begin observing them in their natural environments, you realize that consumers build workarounds to make the tools and products in their lives work more effectively. I have seen sticky notes around computer screens, passwords written in notebooks, chemicals stored dangerously close to each other because they are sorted by task and the dangers are not obvious, and technology devices with added features that make the consumer's life easier but would definitely void the manufacturer's warranty.

Consumers create their own elaborate systems to survive and thrive in their daily environments. If the password for a website is too long or difficult to remember, many will just write it down on a sticky note and attach it on the side of the monitor. Other consumers who view this approach as unsafe would never consider doing this; instead, they might write it down in a notebook and keep it in a locked drawer. This tiny difference in keeping up with a hard-to-remember password is a gaping window into the core of each type of person. More important, these workarounds become talking points for analysis and follow-up with the consumer about unmet needs.

I also identify patterns in the core of who people are by viewing them in the context of where they spend their lives. For example, someone may claim to be a neat person and appear as such in public. Yet when you see piles of paper stacked on that same person's desk and pouring out of their file cabinets, you learn so much more.

The truth is that consumers lie—every single one of us. We don't do it on purpose; it's simply part of our human nature to present the best sides of ourselves, even if those portrayals aren't completely accurate. But understanding the lie and its intent, getting beneath it to uncover the truth, is what helps you truly understand differences in groups of individuals. There are patterns in these lies that marketers can use to hone their messaging and develop the most desirable products. It's essential to not only speak to who a consumer *wants* to be but also understand who that person really *is*.

A prime example of this is couponing and coupon use. We conducted one particular study during the time that *Extreme Couponing* was popular both as a television show and as a trend. We kept hearing from a group of people who were planning to extreme coupon at some point. Of course, this was merely an aspiration. We ended up calling this group *casual couponers*—people who would participate in coupons only if they happened upon them. We could tell that they weren't as serious about couponing based on other contextual cues: how they kept their houses and how they approached other life goals such as weight loss or saving money. All these goals were something this cluster aspired to do, but they just didn't have the motivation (and more important, the encouragement) to accomplish them. They didn't have the core DNA necessary to be true extreme couponers.

The same study exposed us to a group of people who had a highly systematic approach to using coupons. They clipped coupons regularly and used them effectively—and this organized approach extended to areas of their life beyond coupon use. But they wouldn't engage in *extreme* couponing, because they saw it for what it was: organized hoarding.

The Inadequacy of Focus Groups

I often encounter companies trying to use focus groups or similar methods to get to an underlying understanding of their consumers and determine what products or messages to build for them. Despite their widespread use, focus groups are fraught with issues, for many reasons. They are an overused and, quite frankly, lazy technique to get to the type of information that is necessary for product development and messaging in the new world.

Many companies assume that they've recruited a group of "like" people in a focus group, but how do you truly know how alike they are? Just because a certain group shares a demographic characteristic or segmentation, or even if they have bought or might likely buy similar items in the future, isn't a *guarantee* that their motivation and core drivers are similar in any way.

Another big danger with focus groups is that many companies skimp on recruiting the right number of groups to ensure accurate patterns. If something happens to your only focus group or even one of the three focus groups you are conducting, you lose all of the data from that group. But if something happens in an individual interview, you lose only the data from that one individual. And no matter how skilled or experienced a focus group moderator is, there are things that can and *do* happen during focus groups that affect the outcome. You can have an unruly participant, or the moderator may ask a question the wrong way or out of order. Once something like this occurs, you have a much larger problem than the loss of a single interview.

Other limitations are that these groups don't allow for individual discovery with the participants. You can't get to the heart of what a participant's words *truly* mean, because it's difficult and awkward to probe them on the root issue in front of others.

The list of drawbacks goes on. There are time limits; it's an artificial environment; and there is groupthink, dominance issues, and a social pecking order. The very format of a focus group defeats its primary purpose: to get a deep understanding of the individuals in the room. To do that, you need to spend time with each one of them. But if you divide the amount of time spent in a focus group (on average 1½ hours) by the number of participants, you really only "hear" from each participant for about 12 minutes total.

I do believe that focus groups have a place; however, it comes *after* you've completed the proper work to truly understand who the consumer groups are. Once you know that, you can identify these individuals predictably through behavioral and motivational questions that get to their core. Then you can recruit a group of truly like people to help with ideation or evaluation of product concepts and marketing messages.

It is far better to hear six individuals describe something individually than listen to a group of six in a room. When individuals describe the same problem or express the same need while you speak with them one on one—*without* influence from others in a room—you know that you've found a pattern. And when you can predict what a person is going to say, either by contextual cues or because of prior responses, you know that it's a pattern that you can capitalize on.

I avoid the "warm body to fill a seat" approach that many firms use to recruit participants. Instead, I use recruiting techniques that focus on consumers' behaviors, attitudes, and context. I use standard demographics such as income, age range, or gender to map to our client's segmentation to satisfy the marketers in the room—and to prove to them that demographics just don't matter. An ideal participant is someone who has "never participated in anything like this before."

You Cannot Use Online Surveys to Conduct True Laddering

If focus groups are not the best approach to laddering, then online surveys certainly aren't either. They present their own set of problems for conducting research overall. For instance, how do you know the right person is even taking the survey? How do you know the question is the right question? Even the best survey writer can craft a confusing or misinterpreted question, and the online survey environment doesn't allow for follow-up. You should use this research technique only when you're confirming what you already know. Never *ever* use it for exploratory research.

I have talked with many people who admit to flying through the survey to get the $5 at the end to use for shopping at their favorite merchant. These participants have no vested interest in providing thoughtful responses; they simply see it as a "time is money" proposition and often complete the surveys while engaging in other tasks. They know how to answer the questions to get into the database and participate in as many surveys as possible, and they're much more interested in quantity than quality. Do you really want to base the future of your brand on the responses of someone who is willing to complete a 20-minute survey for $5?

If discussing this compensation in the context of demographics, does this even fit with what your demographic or segmentation studies tell you your consumers earn for the same amount of time?

I uncover further evidence against using online surveys in the laddering processes itself. You will learn while laddering your consumers that there are groups that will *never* participate in an online survey. And they may very well be a part of the consumer group that you need to reach most, maybe even your biggest opportunity. How can you continue to create products and services if you're ignoring the most critical group's primary avenue for sharing feedback and desires?

I can get these very people to participate in a conversation when I take the time to establish a relationship with them. In fact, relationship is what drives these groups and keeps them from participating in surveys. By taking the time to connect with these groups in the manner and environment they wish, I am able to hear *all* the voices, not just those willing to participate in anonymous surveys. I want and need to talk to these people to get a complete picture of what will and will not work when conducting a proper laddering study.

As we move even further into a relationship-based society, we have to consider the following: Why would consumers think you care if you are not willing to sit down with them in their environments and truly *understand* who they are and what they want? Compare this with the process of buying a present for someone for his or her birthday or a holiday. The best gifts always come from a true understanding of what's important, dear, and core to the receiver. The consumer who is spending money with your company deserves and expects the same level of respect and understanding.

Start with What You Already Know

Understand that I am not proposing that you throw out everything you have ever done when undertaking a laddering project. You should most definitely use existing knowledge about your customer base as a starting point. You have been successful making sales to groups of people over a given period of time, so you know your approach is not completely wrong. It's just not enough to survive long term or to make significant strides in product innovation and marketing strategy.

I go into every laddering project using the information a company can already tell me about its consumers. I use demographics, life stage, or other segmentation information that's been derived from the company's big data sources as a starting point or a hypothesis. I just don't assume that this knowledge is important or the hypothesis is accurate to the consumer's decision-making process until I hear the consumer tell me so or I understand it from the patterns I uncover in the consumer's behavior.

Starting with existing knowledge allows you to begin to uncover what works or what doesn't. It provides a common language, a bridge between existing knowledge about the consumer and what is learned during the laddering process.

In the next chapter, I will discuss the discrete steps you must take to properly perform laddering from the right perspective: that of your *consumer*, not your product, service, company, or brand.

Key Points

- Thomas J. Reynolds and Jonathan Gutman introduced laddering based on Means-End Theory. Their approach states that product attributes lead to consequences that generate personal meaning (values) for users.
- When mass production was the common approach, brands performed laddering on their products to understand key features. The marketer started with the product and worked to understand how to make the consumer buy the product by appealing to a higher-order need such as fitting in or being seen as cool by others.
- To build products for your consumers today, you need to understand what they want. Only by understanding their core drivers can you become an architect of a product, service, or experience that will resonate with your end consumers.
- Consumers need a concrete idea or concept to react to, much like the architectural plans for a house. They will not be able to ideate for you, but they can react to what you show them.
- Focus groups and online surveys are not a proper shortcut to understanding your consumers. They do not allow you to get to the core of each individual who is participating in the research, and the very nature of the techniques introduce bias.
- Laddering doesn't require you to begin completely from scratch. You can start with what you already know about consumers from the work you've already done with them. Just don't analyze the results with these patterns until you confirm their validity with the actual source: the consumers themselves.

Cruise Line Case Study

By this point in the book, you should begin to understand how crucial it is for marketers and product managers to take a new approach to their interactions with consumers. Specifically, they must move from focusing on trying to sell what they've already built to instead building what the consumer wants. You'll recall from the BellSouth example that we were looking for the core behaviors and drivers that compelled consumers to want a given product. The following case study provides a clear example of how laddering your consumers can help you ensure you are using the right words for marketing and promotion.

Several years ago, we were commissioned to conduct a study for a high-end cruise line. The company had informed us that baby boomer–aged women (those born between 1946 and 1964) were the most common purchasers and drivers behind cruise purchases. In fact, the cruise company was so sure that this was *the* demographic for the cruise purchase that our contacts wouldn't allow us to talk with any other demographic group and they wanted to make sure they had a large enough sample. Although we would typically talk to about 18 respondents for a study of this nature, we instead talked to 35 baby boomer women, all cruisers who were geographically, economically, and ethnically dispersed.

These women told us about everything—from their divorces, to hot flashes, to struggles with rearing self-sufficient children. One respondent even shared with us the story of having one of her toes shortened because of the pain it caused her in wearing high heels. This is a powerful example of how, when done properly, laddering can break through people's standard defenses,

(continued)

(continued)

thereby providing you with more information than you would ever get through traditional research methods, because you spend your time seeking to truly understand the consumer.

The cruise line expected us to find certain tenets of the boomer woman's life that it could then use to create a website filled with content specifically for them. They had already adopted an image of the boomer woman who finds her independence as she enters into the middle part of her life. As a result, they anticipated hearing about themes such as empowerment, family, being in the prime of one's life, and a newfound freedom as an empty nester.

They also believed that boomer women would be very worried about the location of their cabin and that they would want extensive diagrams of the ship to make them feel safe. They assumed these consumers would want to know that they were near elevators in case they needed to disembark during an emergency or if they were returning to their room alone. This information would drive the content that would appeal to and generate the leads for a new website.

If we had followed the old-school way of laddering—by starting with cruise ship's features—we would have ended up building a prioritized list of ship features and then presenting them along with how each of the features made the boomer woman feel. The website would promote the highest-order features of the ship along with a message that would resonate with these women as it relates to time of their life. Let's say, for example, that the order of importance started with being on a new ship. Messaging might have been, "Have the time of your life as you cruise on our newest ship!"

But fortunately for the cruise line we didn't take this approach. Instead, we used a broader lens to truly understand what made these people decide to take a cruise vacation and select the line they did. As we started to analyze the results and uncover the patterns after the interviews, we found that there's not really a set of best practices or guiding principles that drives a boomer woman to make this choice. In fact, there was nothing special about being a boomer or a woman for this decision. And although we did hear about empowerment, family, and being in the prime of their life, security was not at the forefront of the decision criteria. If we had brought it up artificially, it would automatically have become important (as happens in much qualitative research, especially online surveys), and we would have gotten a false-positive result on this being an item that was crucial to emphasize. Who is going to say that safety isn't important?

We learned there are three different clusters that matter in the context of deciding to go on a cruise vacation: destination, party, and leisure (Figure 3.1).

Figure 3.1   There Are Three Major Factors in Deciding to Take a Cruise Vacation: Destination, Party and Leisure

(continued)

(continued)

DESTINATION

Some people choose a cruise based on the destination that the ship is headed to. They really don't care about the ship as long as they have food and a place to sleep. They never want to travel to the same location twice; they want their passport stamped often in as many exotic locales as possible. This group wouldn't care if a company put its worst ship on its most exotic location; they are simply using the ship as a taxicab to get to the location they really want to see.

PARTY

For other people, cruising is all about the party. In fact, they are very likely to cruise on the same ship (or route) every year with the same people. They want a ship that has a variety and number of discos, dance clubs, bars, casinos, and onboard activities. They care about their room, but only in terms of whether they can find it, because they really don't plan on spending a lot of time there. They will travel on the newest ship on the same route.

LEISURE

The last major cluster we identified was a group that takes a cruise for the pampering and the leisure. They spend their days lounging by the pool, visiting the spa, and enjoying all five courses of dinner as they gaze out the dining room window. They prefer to spend their time with a select few and love a ship that has all the latest leisurely amenities—a new spa treatment and several pools and hot tubs—essentially requiring a high lounge chair-to-cruiser ratio.

We would have completely missed the mark if we had only concentrated on building best practices or guiding principles for this customer set without laddering. We had to understand the motivations and behaviors behind why people choose to cruise and why they were choosing to cruise with this specific cruise line. The company needed to make their website's structure and content different for each cluster to truly be successful and maximize the experience.

By supplying the right content, users would self-select into the content that really mattered to them. For the destination group, we recommended including glossy pictures of exotic lands; for the party people, highlighting the casinos and clubs, their locations onboard, and a schedule of activities; and for the leisure-focused group, posting pictures of lounging couples in bathrobes that highlighted the latest spa treatment or advancement.

We didn't have to ask any specific questions such as, "Why do you travel?" to get them to make this selection. In addition, we could avoid using the standard boring, ineffective cruise selector that is on most cruise and travel sites. We also had to understand that a party person might be married or influenced by someone who was focused on leisure or destination. The site needed to provide content and architecture that allows the primary researcher to find the things he or she wants while highlighting information relevant to the secondary traveler.

Thankfully, the cruise line gave us the latitude to understand these women more deeply. Too often the marketer or researcher is ready to just get to the point, which only causes them to miss the point altogether.

(continued)

(continued)

By taking the time to examine the broader definition of this segmentation, we were we able to understand consumers different motivations and behaviors—the answer behind *why* people choose to cruise. The purpose of laddering is to answer why. Why are consumers acting, reacting, or participating? Tapping into the true motivations is the only way to define and then measure true success.

In the next chapter, we will get down to brass tacks on what steps to take to ladder consumers properly.

4

The Steps to Laddering

Why do you wear a mask? Were you burned by acid or something?

Oh no, it's just they're terribly comfortable. I think everyone will be wearing them in the future.

—The Princess Bride

WHETHER WE REALIZE it or not, we put on a mask every morning as we head out into the world. Some of us wear the mask of successful business owner, while some present ourselves as teachers, skaters, doting mothers, or renegades.

We create an external identity of who we are, and we are careful to present ourselves that way as we go about our daily tasks. We use our clothing, appearance, and speech to communicate this identity to others.

Yet who we present ourselves to be in public is *very* different from what others might observe about us if watching us in our most intimate of places, such as our homes, cars, and offices, or even if looking through our bags and purses. It takes getting into these intimate places—beyond the mask we present—to understand who we really are underneath. And as we move even further into the era of the acceptance of the individual, we choose to buy from and associate with brands that resonate with who we are at our core. We avoid those that try to sell to us or change our fundamental behavior.

In his book *Blink* (2007), author Malcolm Gladwell introduces and discusses the concept of *thin slicing*. In my experience, this is a much faster way to get an idea of a person's core than simply listening to what that person tells you, especially if that person has been paid to come to an unfamiliar environment or participate in an artificial scenario, as often is the case in focus groups or a lab-based study.

Gladwell cites a study in which people had the option of understanding others by either going out with them twice a week for over a year (for example, every Saturday night to dinner and out to lunch) or spending just 30 minutes walking through their bedrooms. Of course, both common sense and our bias tell us that spending *more*

67

time with a person would be much more revealing than just a short visit to his or her bedroom. But the study revealed the opposite: the people who spent only 30 minutes in someone's bedroom learned and understood more about the person they were evaluating than those who spent time with the actual person. They were able to gather important information about the individual that they might not have ever picked up in a more public, social setting.

This is the result of a double-blindness. We present ourselves to others a certain way, and it's within our nature to accept another person for what he or she presents. The more time we spend with that person, the more we carry this belief and the harder it is for us to see and accept that person as something different.

This explains why many shows and movies focus on the person with the double identity or the character who leads a double life: *Nurse Jackie, Dexter*, Don Draper from *Mad Men*, and even our heroes Batman, Superman, and Spider-Man. We are fascinated by who they present themselves to be versus who they *really* are—because we all know that we do the same thing in our own way.

This is why, to do it effectively, we must perform laddering in context, that is, when and where the consumer uses the product, makes the buying decision, or uses a service.

Context provides us with a deeper understanding that tells us more than what the person is saying outwardly while we're conducting the laddering conversation. It's this information—getting behind what is being said or done—that's so crucial to a truly successful evaluation.

At this point, I am focusing on evaluating a product or tangible experience. I know that you may be reading this book for marketing messaging and content, and I promise that I'm getting there. To succeed with the marketing message part of the process, you must start with something concrete that the consumer can understand and tell you. People know how to react to concrete questions and ideas; they know how to tell you about their lives and how they lead them, and they can share what's important to them. Yet most individuals have rarely, if ever, spent time contemplating *why* these things are important or what the underlying need is they are seeking to fulfill.

By taking the time to truly understand your consumers, you can start speaking to them at a place of understanding. As a result, you can build products, services, messaging, and experiences that resonate with consumers in ways they can't even explain. Some of the world's most admired brands, such as Apple, Target, Old Navy, Harley Davidson, and Starbucks, have perfected this by becoming a brand consumers want to hang out with, just like they do with their other friends.

This chapter will provide some practical advice on how to understand your consumer more deeply than you ever have before. I will give you some guiding principles on how to successfully conduct laddering with your consumers to ensure you are getting to a foundational and pure understanding. This advice is relevant beyond laddering—it applies any time you have a conversation with someone—professionally or personally. Always strive to understand what really matters to the other person in a given situation or context.

Step 1: Have a Broad Conversation

Instead of laddering the product by starting with a features or function set, you want to ladder the *consumer*. So you must start broadly. If you begin by immediately taking a consumer to the product's feature level, it's impossible to bring that person out more broadly to understand what really drives him or her in terms of context or choice along the decision journey.

One of the biggest mistakes I see people make with the laddering technique or qualitative research in general is starting too intently focused on the topic at hand. They begin conversations with something like this: "Today, we are going to talk to you about how you choose to travel" or "I want to show you some new concepts for a technology product." When you narrow the conversation into a particular context from the very start, the consumer immediately starts to play the game and begins performing when answering the questions being posed. The consumer may even start trying to guess the right answer.

Often, a marketing manager or high-level executive wants to get straight to the point, but doing so discounts the consumer before the process has even really begun. There's an adage that states, "No one cares what you know unless they know that you care." By starting the conversation broadly, you show you care about the consumer—and you will learn about what comes before and after and what influences the consumer's decision. The really good, interesting stuff, the things you didn't expect to hear, might be the very factors that drive the overall adoption, and they are very likely the difference in success or failure.

So spend some time establishing a base. Learn about who consumers are as people; get to know them, what makes them tick, what makes them worry, and who or what influences their decisions. You won't know if this broad information is important until you start analyzing the data or understanding the relationships between what you are hearing and what the product, service, experience, or solution can offer. But if you don't collect that information during this process, it's impossible to go back and gather it cleanly and meaningfully later.

Step 2: Document Their Environment

I begin evaluating a person's drivers and motivation from the second I pull into their neighborhood or apartment complex and as I walk up to their door or enter their office. I take pictures of their environment. And I use everything that I collect as a clue to whom each person is—and more importantly, who that person wants to be.

I know that I provide the same clues for other people, as do you. As I mentioned earlier, if you visited my office, you would find a collection of Starbucks mugs from all over the world. The average observer might assume that I must really love coffee, especially Starbucks coffee. But what these mugs *truly* represent is my core desire to travel and love of visiting different places. These mugs have become a barometer for me when I meet a salesperson for the first time. Let me tell you how.

I can tell the difference between a good salesperson and a great salesperson by what that person says about these mugs. A good sales guy will say, "I see that you really like Starbucks." But a great sales guy notices that the mugs are from all over the place and will ask something more meaningful, such as, "Did you collect those mugs on your trips, or do other people bring them to you?" The mugs are a little bit about coffee and Starbucks; they are a *lot* about travel, new experiences, and new places. They serve as a reminder of what I really love and what I am ultimately pursuing: the nomadic freedom of a world traveler. A good gift or follow-up for me isn't about coffee (although I won't turn away an offer for someone to pay for my habit). I am far more likely to remember a recommendation someone makes for a place to visit or stay on my pursuit to visit everywhere.

Think about the items you collect or keep on your desk or space at work. What do they say about what is really important to you? Even if you answer, "I keep very little in my office" or "My area is sparsely decorated," that speaks volumes about you as well. It means that you are either (1) not that committed to where you are currently working or (2) have interests elsewhere, something you care about more. You learn as much about others in the absence of participation or information as you do in when they actively participate.

Starting broadly and documenting the consumers' surroundings allows you to fully understand your consumers and how their environment affects them. Our best interviews are those in which the participant says at the end, "I have no idea what you were asking me about, but I hope I was helpful." By keeping the first rounds of conversation broad, we can look for what's really important to the consumer— and what else might be affecting him or her.

Step 3: Talk to Enough Consumers Until You Have Talked to Enough Consumers

The goal here is to understand the patterns in the groups to whom you are talking. I often am asked, "How many interviews do you need to do to accomplish this?"

As I mentioned earlier, the standard answer I give is, "I don't know what I know until I know it." And although that might sound like a nonanswer, it's the truth. If we looked at how we learn anything, that's the case: we don't know that we know something until we know it. And until we can describe and explain it to others with confidence, we are still learning.

You need to interview people until you start hearing and seeing repeated patterns. When you can begin to predict what the person is going to say because of what you have learned previously, you know that you're onto something. When you can explain to others why consumers are behaving a certain way based on a set of certain conditions, you have come to the point of learning and realization.

This might sound ominous, but don't despair. As long as your context is narrow enough (which is always the case if you work for a specific brand or product), you will likely start noticing patterns between 18 and 27 interviews. This means *individual* interviews, not interviews with 18 to 27 people in groups (recall the problems with focus groups that we've already covered). As previously mentioned, focus groups do have a place and can be done effectively but only after you have a base understanding of who your consumers are and what makes them tick. This initial set of interviews allows you to fine-tune your conversation to learn what parts are important and to determine how many more interviews you need to conduct.

Although these numbers might seem small to the quant-minded, that's the beauty of this work. I have proven time and time again that the predicted distribution of the clusters taken from a small sample stands true when quantified. Until we get to a point where we are using the right lens to unlock the big data that we're collecting, quantifying the new connected consumer is going to continue be a tricky proposition unless paired with strong qualitative understanding.

One reason for this is that quantification methods require the consumer to *opt in*—in other words, to participate. And one of the first things you learn when you begin to ladder your consumers is that certain individuals don't participate. And if their core behavior is to not participate, why would you expect them to do so in a survey or process that quantifies them? That's why we must get beyond survey data and counting to an understanding of observed behavior, tone, and intent. This type of information provides a much stronger indicator of who individuals are. Starting with this understanding is a far more compelling reason to collect big data than the mere collection of big data under the assumption that the collection alone will lead to an epiphany.

Step 4: Make Sure You Are Talking to the Right Person (or People)

As you go through the process of laddering, you have to be careful about bias, for example, the paradox of chooser verses user. One can highly influence the other, and unless you know what truly influences the use or buying decision, you may begin working under some inaccurate assumptions.

This was the case when I was conducting a laddering project in the agriculture space regarding tractors. Although one group (the owner) was primarily buying the equipment, another (the operator) was using it. If the buyer was in the room, the operator would always defer to what the buyer said. After all, the buyer was usually the boss and very possibly the owner of the farm or the operation. What could an operator with only a few years of experience possibly know that the boss didn't? Even if the operator thought he or she knew more, it would be disrespectful to express a differing opinion in that setting.

At the same time, the buyer would lament about having purchased equipment the operators complained was too hard to use. Buyers were unlikely to buy this same tractor or tractor line again if the operators didn't accept it. Combine this with the fact that buyers didn't regularly, if ever, actually use the equipment as part of their day-to-day tasks. To get an accurate read of what was important, I had to speak to the operator of the tractor independently of the buyer.

This type of bias occurs in established groups; it's known widely through the qualitative community. If you are working with a vendor who suggests putting work colleagues together in a room to get to the root of a problem, you need to look for a new supplier.

What people do not recognize or discuss as much is that this same bias exists when performing studies or having conversations with strangers who have just met. If focus group participants discuss their professions, either because they are asked or because the topic comes up as part of the natural conversation, an unspoken pecking order is established. Social norms teach us to take our place. If we realize we are in a room with others who might be smarter, wealthier, or better at something than we are, we naturally defer to the dominant person in the room.

This can occur when studies are performed with two parents in a room; each will try to outdo the other by presenting himself or herself as the better, more informed, protective parent. The contextual information we pick up from studies we've conducted on the same topic is far more valuable than what we learn in a pristine environment.

One such study focused on parents' concerns regarding Internet security; in these situations, the children would usually be somewhere in the vicinity as we carried out the interviews. Mom or Dad would tell us about all of the security measures they had put in place to make sure that they had limited their children's access to harmful content or social media channels. Meanwhile, the child would be standing in the background, gleefully sharing with us the workarounds they used to avoid the protective barrier their parents had established. One young lady told me that when her parents restricted access at 9 PM each night, she just hopped onto the neighbor's open network and continued to chat with her friends across Facebook. This is not information I would have gathered by bringing her Mom to a lab facility—and certainly not by putting her Mom in a focus group with other parents. This finding was not the exception either; rather, it became one of the factors that separated parents into different groups.

If you have conducted your laddering work broadly, in the proper context and with the right person, you can explain with finite detail how the clusters relate to each other. I call this process *latticing* the user groups. I will go into deeper detail later in the book in Chapter 6 about how understanding this relation can help you to both target consumers and create additional reach for the products, services, or experiences you are creating.

Step 5: Keep Your Data and Your Information Clean

Always conduct interviews in pairs to make sure you have more than one point of view. This allows you to capture from both a broad *top-down* perspective as well as a detailed *bottom-up* point of view. This approach prevents bias when looking at the data, because one

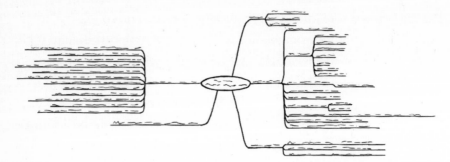

Figure 4.1   Example of a Mind Map of Bottom-Up Data

consumer might be especially memorable and affect the impression of the person leading the conversations.

Team members should fulfill different roles throughout this process. One can conduct the interview, while the other takes detailed notes during each and uses a mind map to cluster findings from the notes, as shown in Figure 4.1.

The team member conducting the interviews should work from the top down, coming up with a list of large topics or themes thought to be important based on the interviewing process (see Figure 4.2).

Not only does this dual approach protect the data, but it allows the interviewer to truly focus on the conversation at hand. And the secondary player (the notetaker) keeps the interviewer honest by ensuring that the interviewer covers all of the same ground with each participant. Of course, you don't need to cover the discussion the same way with each person, because the conversation should flow naturally. However, you do need to pick up the same answers to questions and curiosities either directly or indirectly in your time with the consumer.

Step 6: Keep the Conversation on the Topic at Hand; Avoid Distractions

Money is a good example of a topic that can detract from the root conversation. It's always a consideration; almost every consumer

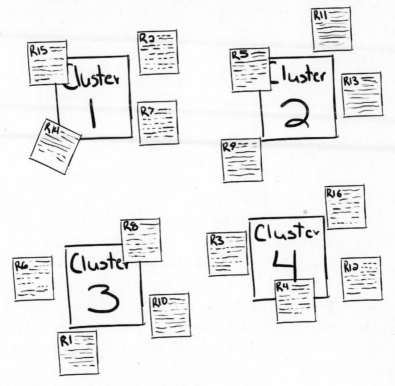

Figure 4.2   Example of Top-Down Patterns

wants to start a conversation about a product, service, or experience with "depending on the price." You have to remove that factor from their consideration and get them to talk about what they *really* care about. Then you can understand how the price might affect their decision. Money affects only how consumers manifest their core. They will find a way to express their core, even if money is currently an issue for them.

We have conducted many laddering projects during economic downturns or uncertainty. As a result, some consumers who worry about how they appear publicly and have a desire to spend as part of their core may not look like they are having any kind of economic issue. But once you get into their house or other private space, you can quickly ascertain what's really going on.

Again, uncovering the real drivers requires that you understand and involve yourself in the consumers' context—their homes, offices, or whatever it is—to get a true picture of what's really going on in their lives. Don't let them, or yourself, get sidetracked by a limiting factor like money.

Step 7: Your Results Should Make Sense at a High Level

The number of clusters is going to be based on the topic that you are covering, otherwise known as *context*. You can use this number of clusters or the repeating patterns of answers, context, behavior, or content as a guidepost to check your work.

Because the context in my earlier examples of cruising or banking is very small, the number of clusters is also very small: three. The cluster size grows to six in the case of the intersection of social media and TV in the upcoming case study because both of those contexts are very large.

We can use coffee as an example of a good way to think about how many clusters (distinct consumer groups that map to one another because of their core DNA or behavior) might exist. The number of clusters for people who drink coffee would be large, something like seven to nine. The number of people who go out for coffee or buy it on their way into work verses brewing and drinking it at home would be smaller, closer to four to six. And the number of clusters of consumers who stop at a specific type of coffee location would be more like two or three.

Isn't it great to think that you only really need to manage two or three groups within a discrete brand or experience—and that you can speak to these people in a way that's really important and meaningful to them? As we move into the next chapter, we will get into the brass tacks of how to perform a laddering exercise that unlocks and uncovers your consumers' core drivers and behaviors.

Key Points

- We all wear masks, that is, present ourselves differently in public than we truly are in private or when we're with those who know us best.
- Have a broad conversation with your consumers to peel away their masks. Start by understanding the person, then move closer in to the product or subject at hand.
- Pay close attention not only to what the consumer tells you but also to what isn't shared. There are many clues to who consumers are and what is important to them buried in the context of where they live.
- Have enough conversations with consumers until you start to see repeating patterns in the answers. Once you can predict what a consumer is going to say based on that person's previous answers or contextual clues, you know you are starting to catch on to what's important to a group.
- Often, companies will focus on the wrong person in the buying or choosing equation. By paying attention to the context you are in and the information you are collecting, you can uncover these biases and consider them when evaluating the results.
- Perform your conversations with consumers in pairs. Have one person focus on collecting information from the bottom and mapping it while the other person thinks about the big picture and works from the top down.
- Avoid introducing information that could skew your results; money, for example, is always a part of the conversation but is rarely the real driving factor behind a consumer's buying decision.
- The number of clusters you uncover should map to the size of the context. If the topic you are discussing with the consumers is very narrow, you will have only a handful of clusters. A broader topic such as television will have a much larger set of clusters.

The Social TV Case Study

We are always curious to understand how different technologies are disrupting the world around us. Recently, there's been a great deal of conversation about second screen experiences, that is, the use of an alternate screen (think laptop, tablet, or mobile phone) while viewing a primary screen (think television). There's a particular focus on what people were doing within this trend. We kept hearing companies and reports concentrate too specifically on the *what* regarding second screen usage:

1. How many times *people mentioned a brand*
2. How many times *an application had been downloaded*

To fully understand the mind-set of users at the intersection of social media and television, we did what we do best: spent hours interviewing people in their homes and watching them watch television. Nothing paints a truer picture than seeing someone in their own environment using technology the way they usually would. By observing this, we were able to discover the true reason why consumers were participating in social media and using technology on second screens while watching television.

Because the definition of social media has and will continue to change as the technology evolves and changes, we used a very broad definition. Our definition included having conversations with others in the room; sending text messages; posting information to Twitter, Facebook, or other public social media platforms; and using applications that support primary screen viewership and communication among the viewers.

We compiled the information in an attempt to uncover the true and important patterns. As a result, we came up with five primary and one "in-context" clusters at the intersection of social media and television use. There are clusters that exist in the TV-only section and the social media–only section. But because we were looking only at clusters that we found at the intersection of the two, we ignored the clusters that fell into these categories. They were irrelevant to our focus on the point of where social media and television converged.

Figure 4.3 helps explain how the clusters relate to one another and depicts something known as *a lattice*. The

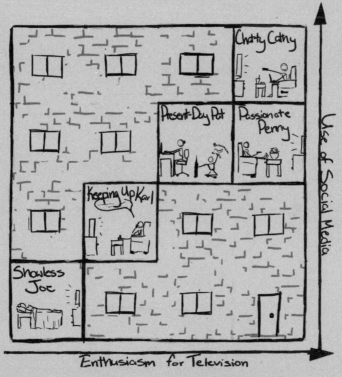

Figure 4.3 The Convergence of Social Media and Television Viewing

(continued)

(continued)

clusters shown in the figure's lower left corner (Showless Joe) care very little about television or social media; however, they do participate some in both. The clusters in the upper right use television and social media, but you will find as you read their narrative that it's for very different reasons.

SHOWLESS JOE

The first social TV user that falls at the lowest part of the continuum is Showless Joe. Joe is not a TV guy, and he doesn't really understand the attraction to much of what is on television. He turns on the television when he wants something mindless to do or is looking for background noise. If he is paying attention, he is most likely watching the news or something educational on the History Channel or TLC. He drives others in the room crazy because he is never worried about seeing the end of a show. He watches his television live; he thinks that using a DVR is just too much of a commitment and spending the time to set one up doesn't synch with his belief that TV is a waste of time. Once a commercial comes on, he simply switches to a different station and watches another show, wherever it happens to pick up.

You will likely find Joe dozing in front of the television, because he uses it primarily as white noise to help him fall asleep.

Joe's enthusiasm for social media is equal to that for television. He knows what social media is but views it as self-promoting and a potential privacy risk. He prefers direct communication with others over the phone or, ideally, in person.

At first glance, you might not think Joe is important to the convergence of social media and television. However, it's just as important to understand who you are *not* targeting as it is to understand who you are. Joe is not likely to change his interest or his behavior to conform; therefore, you must conform to *him*. The best and most effective way to appeal to him within television programming would be to use methods that emphasize in-person interaction, venues such as sports bars, stadiums, or other places people gather to interact.

KEEPING UP KARL

We called the second cluster we uncovered during the research *Keeping Up Karl*. Karl is interested in television and social media but solely as a means to stay connected on a personal level with people in his life he cares about.

By watching the same shows as his family and friends, Karl feels included, relevant, and as though he can contribute to the conversation. He loves watching *American Idol* or the latest episode of *Modern Family* so that he's aware of current gossip or the latest jokes. He uses social media sites such as Facebook to get updates on what those he loves are doing. He rarely posts anything but is sure to comment on, like, and lurk on what other people are posting.

Karl feels the same way about technology in general. He most likely uses a feature phone and realizes that text messaging and other electronic communications are the way to go if he wants to stay connected with his younger family members. He watches his television live; he never really figured out his VCR and can't imagine he would be more successful with a DVR. He definitely knows when certain shows are on and is

(continued)

(*continued*)

sure to be in front of the TV to stay up to date. As far as Karl is concerned, the most important aspect of television is using it as a way to keep connected to those that he loves. Similarly, he uses social media as a way for them to remember him.

Cluing Karl in on what is popular and new helps him keep up with his family. He would appreciate an application or a system that lets him know what is popular among different groups, especially with those that he cares most about. He wants to be able to have a relevant conversation and appear to be up on the latest entertainment.

PRESENT-DAY PAT

The best way to describe Present-Day Pat is busy. She has hobbies and errands that keep her out and about, not at home in front of her TV set. She has places to go and people to see, but there are definitely some shows she likes and wants to keep up with. She loves the fact that her DVR lets her have it all. She can record her favorite shows and watch them when she has some down time, usually on the weekend or on a weeknight when she has nothing else planned.

Her social media usage must be mobile; she needs and wants to be able to text, tweet, and update Facebook on the run. In fact, since she got her iPad, she can't remember the last time she sat in front of her laptop for an extended period of time except to pay bills. Her posts focus on what she's doing and where she's going. They're all about her real life *outside* of technology and certainly television.

Pat loves that so many of her shows are now available for streaming to her phone, tablet, and laptop. She uses this feature to sneak in a few minutes of her favorite shows while waiting to pick the kids up at ballet practice or tee ball. This capability has allowed her to start watching a new show her friend just told her about, even if she is a couple of seasons behind. Who watches shows live and on the night they premiere anymore anyway? Pat is especially excited that many of the streaming services are gaining access to content first—now she can entertain her kids on long road trips with the latest movie from Disney, Pixar, and other quality sources.

When Pat watches television at home, she uses technology in a completely different way for something different than what is on the television screen, such as completing a project for work or looking up a set of recipes on Pinterest for the coming week.

Pat would be lost without access to her social media channels and entertainment while on the go. She's not sure how we ever lived without the instant access we have now to everyone and everything.

To make Pat happy, make sure you provide her with all of your content. She is not concerned about being the first to watch something or often even worried about watching a show in sequence. Your content must be available in a mobile way; she should be able to access it on the go, not just via her television screen.

PASSIONATE PENNY

The next cluster can be found comfortably ensconced every night on their favorite couch. Passionate Penny wants to watch as much television as possible. She has dedicated TV time almost every night and considers television and many channels of entertainment to be a hobby and favorite pastime.

(continued)

(continued)

Penny DVRs *everything*; this allows her to fast-forward through all commercials and filler fluff to get straight to the meat of the show. Why waste an hour watching the season finale of *Survivor* or a results show on *American Idol*, she figures, when the really important part takes place during the last 10 minutes?

Penny is the queen of her remote control and knows all the shortcuts to maximize her TV viewing experience. She uses social media to support her TV viewing and loves that her technology lets her in on all the behind the scenes information, all the gossip on her favorite actors. She follows her favorite celebrities on Twitter and is delighted when Facebook gives her the inside scoop. She whips her phone out when she thinks she recognizes an actor from another movie or TV show to look them up and satisfy her curiosity.

Penny loves season premieres more than any other time of the year. She is reluctant to move to a noncable solution because she worries that she might miss out on something new. She watches as many new shows as possible and is often surprised (and a little upset) when they get cancelled; she is not watching them live, and they suddenly disappear from her DVR queue. She wants to watch her shows in sequence from beginning to end; the characters and story lines are important to her enjoyment of the show.

You want to provide Penny with something that makes her feel special, a behind the scenes story or access to information about a character or an actor to keep her engaged an intrigued. It's not about her; it's about these characters and shows that she relates to. An application or website that makes her feel like an insider speaks to her core drivers.

CHATTY CATHY

The final permanent cluster we uncovered we call Chatty Cathy. Social media is a cocktail party to Cathy—and she loves to party. She uses television shows and events as conversation starters but moves on to the next trending topic once the buzz dies down. She sees herself as an authority or the go-to person for answers, and social media is just the platform to promote that. As far as she's concerned, the most important person in her social media network is her. Her favorite shows include the Grammys or the Oscars; these give her a chance to shine and allow her to participate in the larger conversation by commenting on what the celebrities are wearing on the red carpet. She also participates in any other trending topic, like what the host of the Super Bowl party she is attending might be serving.

Cathy uses social media to follow other people she knows—not necessarily from real life, but people who she has met over social media and with whom she has established some type of connection. She has no problem broadcasting where she is, what she's eating, or what she thinks. She doesn't find much interest in following other celebrities, because she views herself as a celebrity—and unless they promote her in some way, they are of no use to her.

To win, make Cathy feel like a superstar. Retweet, like, or comment on her posts to keep her engaged. If you promote her, she will promote you. Don't expect Cathy to continue to participate in a conversation about your show beyond an initial push if there is nothing in it for her. Her propensity to follow a trend will skew the "what" data you are collecting about a particular entertainment property. And keep in mind

(continued)

(*continued*)

that you must exclude counting her in the overall pool unless this secondary screen interaction is consistent and continues to push her agenda: promoting herself.

There was one more additional cluster we identified as we went throughout the research. We call this an "in-text" cluster that is transitional. A transitional cluster is composed of a group of consumers who show up only during certain contexts (a time period or because of an event, for example). The final cluster is seasonal, just like your favorite sport. His name is Singular Sam.

SINGULAR SAM

As we were conducting research during football season, we started to look at the use of applications for Fantasy Football. During this research, we stumbled upon an in-context persona, that is, one that exists only for a small period of time when some outside influence affects their standard core behavior. We called this cluster Singular Sam, because they have a singular interest that changes both their social media and television viewing habits.

We noticed that some of our other clusters less interested in TV—Showless Joe and Keeping Up Karl, for example—exhibited an interesting behavior during football season.

When football, especially one of their teams, was on, they were as passionate as Penny about watching. They also enjoyed using social media, but only within their football tribe to talk smack. They preferred private channels, because they didn't consider what they shared to be for public consumption. They were no more likely to post to Facebook (what if their team lost the next week?), but they had no problem ribbing their friends who rooted for opposing teams across private social media backchannels. As soon as football is over, they revert back to their core behavior of either watching very little television or they watch just in support of staying current with friends and family.

The great thing about in-context personas is that they represent a way to get to a group you wouldn't usually be able to access. Giving them something of value that includes hooks to content after the season is over, such as a Fantasy Football application that includes postseason content, is a great way to keep them as a customer during the times that television or social media are not as important. If your channel or application provides replays of games in the off-season or a sneak peak at the upcoming season, there is a reason for this group to continue to participate and revisit the application or experience during that time.

As you can see from this research, the uses of technology while watching television is not just about the *what* that is happening on the television or a secondary screen. A Chatty Cathy can greatly skew a show's perceived success by merely choosing to participate in the conversation just because others are talking. Getting behind the conversation and understanding who is talking (and why) is the only way to truly unlock why consumers are behaving the way they are.

5

Confirming and Fine-Tuning Your Ladders

The only relevant test of validity of a hypothesis is a comparison of prediction with experience.

—Milton Friedman

WE MAY NOT consciously realize it, but we move through our days testing hypotheses that we believe to be true. We awake each morning to the hypothesis that the sun will be in the sky, that we will have air to breathe, and that there will be water when we turn on the faucet. This reliance on hypotheses is how we are fundamentally wired from the days when we had to survive as cavemen (and cavewomen). Our prior experience drives our belief of what will happen in the future. Therefore, it often takes a dramatic change in our experience to alter our hypothesis about the world around us.

Take, for example, the refrigerator in my kitchen. I had lived in my current home for almost 10 years when the filtered water built into the refrigerator door stopped working. I drink many glasses of water every day and cannot break myself from the habit of getting ice from the door and then attempting to get water from the neighboring compartment. My experience of getting water from the refrigerator door is so ingrained that my brain won't give up the hypothesis of also going to the refrigerator for water.

This kind of internal wiring is part of why we have a problem with looking at the world around us in a deeper and more meaningful way. It is what limits marketers' and product development groups' thinking. They continue to use what has worked for them in the past to create new marketing messages, products, and experiences—and who can blame them? Those old ways worked for more than 100 years. But they're attempting to use the old techniques in a changed economy with a changed consumer. It's like trying to use a telegram instead of sending a text message to deliver important news.

To prove that you have gathered relevant and actionable information during the laddering process—that you have identified real clusters—you need to reverse the equation. You must start with some hypothesis about how the clusters you have uncovered will react to

93

an idea, product, message, or experience, and then do some work to find out if this is true. Once you can predict how your consumers naturally react you can train your teams to the idea of thinking from the consumer's point of view instead of their own (called *leasing*).

Once you have completed your initial round of interviews and established your core groups, you'll probably get the feeling that you "know something" or that you are catching on to some kind of pattern. You should move your laddering work forward by making assumptions about the type of stimulus to which these groups will react and why.

This stimulus can come from a wide range of sources: something you have created, something from your competition, or even an example from far outside of your existing scope. This is a great time to get other team members involved in the process and do some blue-sky work with them to generate ideas.

Blue-Sky Brainstorming

In blue-sky work, you throw out a theme, idea, or category and blue-sky—or brainstorm—ideas around it with a cross-functional team. So, for example, let's say that you are building a website for new mothers. One of your categories might be pregnancy. If you want to build a new digital experience for planning for college, you might use a topic such as savings or even ones as simple as planning and then college. Be careful not to narrow the topic too much from the outset. You can always overlap the ideas and narrow them down, but it is very difficult to broaden an idea.

I recommend a cross-functional team, members of your marketing department, development, customer service, quality assurance, and even human resources for this process, because they bring different perspectives and interactions with your consumers to the table. They are experts at potential ideas because they have seen a wide scope, not only of what the company has attempted to do in the past, but also about what competitors might be doing in the space. When doing a blue-sky activity, there are some rules that are important to follow to keep the creative juices flowing:

- There are no bad ideas.
- Every idea gets written down and put up on the board or the wall.
- Discussion about why an idea or solution won't work is not allowed.
- No one is permitted to judge an idea.
- Everyone must contribute.

My favorite way to do this type of activity is to use a blank wall or whiteboard and then write each idea down on a sticky note. I often use different colors to represent *things we have done, things our competitors have done, and/or things from other places.*

I was working with one particular client to build a product that focused on people who typically fell in a lower income bracket. I brainstormed some of the constraints that these people faced using the overall topic of stress relief. One concept that someone suggested was gun ranges. I was tempted to break my rule of don't judge an idea but am glad I didn't. Although gun ranges didn't become the thing included in the offering, it *did* lead us to understand that, at their core, this group was driven by *access*. When this lower-income cluster was presented with the concept of gun ranges, they would talk about how they had never been to one before.

Once we learned this, we were able to create a way for these consumers to access spa packages and other experiences that were usually beyond their reach. We unlocked newfound knowledge by developing a true understanding of one of the groups' core issues: access to experiences or ways to relieve stress.

This revelation also clarified an aspect of the study that had previously confused us. Although many of these lower-income respondents lived in houses with little or no furniture, they did have a large flat-screen TV, Blu-ray player, and the latest gaming system. We began to understand that what many see as frivolous spending was this lower-income group's attempt to relieve stress. It was far cheaper in the long run to buy an at-home entertainment system than it was to go out to the movie theater or bowling alley on any given weekend.

Once your group has created its wall of ideas, sort them by the initial cluster sets, putting ideas under the clusters that the group believes is most appropriate for the proposed idea. For example, if you have created a list of ideas for a new vacation package, sorting the ideas by cluster will help you decide what you want to show each cluster. It's not a problem if an idea seems to fall into two clusters; just make another sticky note and put it under both clusters.

The final step in the blue-skying process is to make your cross-functional team vote. A good rule of thumb is to give each team member votes equal to 10 percent of the ideas; that is, if you generate 100 ideas, everyone gets 10 votes; 150 ideas means that everyone gets 15. I use stars or dots to make this process interactive, and it provides a strong visual impact. The surviving ideas will stand out under each cluster and become the concepts and ideas (artifacts) you will try out with the clusters as you begin confirmation.

Talk to the Expert—the Consumer—to Confirm the Clusters

After you have a prioritized list of artifacts to try out with your clusters, now is the time to talk with your consumers once again.

This second round is when you really start to fine-tune your groups, prove or disprove that they actually exist, and understand more completely what's driving their behavior. This stage is important; it's where the consumers are reacting to concrete concepts. As a result, you'll start to see how those reactions relate to your hypotheses about the groups.

Don't stop learning at this point. Make sure you still have very broad discussions. You should wait to present any and all artifacts until the conversation's end. As you are talking with the consumer, you should be thinking about which group of artifacts you are going to present based on the conversation and in what cluster you believe the consumer fits. The reaction to the artifacts will distinctly divide the groups into one cluster or another. You need to be able to explain why two groups that you believe to be distinctly different from each other both react to a given artifact positively.

Although I always start by testing with the things I think will most likely fit the cluster I believe the consumer fits in, I purposefully continue by presenting content or artifacts that I believe will work with other groups to see how far I can push the cluster one way or another. While making sure that I really understand my clusters and their core drivers, I am also trying to figure out if there's a way to transition them across from one set of artifacts to another. For example, we know that Showless Joe claims to not watch television or use social media that often. By talking with him about some of the artifacts that are more appropriate to the other clusters, we started to learn about Singular Sam and understand under what conditions he would participate in these more engaging experiences.

It's important to pay close attention to both what your consumers tell you and what they leave out. A good clue to whether or not an artifact is relevant to a given consumer is to watch for answers such a, "I might do that one day" or "I have thought about doing that." These are dead giveaways that an artifact isn't for that person and doesn't fit within his or her current or even future behavior. Make sure you are really listening to what the consumer is telling you beyond the spoken answers to your questions. A good follow-up is, "Have you ever done this before?" or "Under what circumstances would you do this?"

Recall the earlier example in Chapter 3 about extreme couponing. A response of "I am thinking about doing it" clearly indicated a lack of sincerity by one of our clusters to perform serious couponing—or even their likelihood to participate in a sweepstakes or giveaway. They wanted to do it, but they never really would; it was just too much trouble. Unless the coupon was in the checkout line or on the grocery store aisle, it was not something that fit within this cluster's core behavior. But because a core component of this group's *consumer DNA* was a strong desire to be liked and affirmed, it was important to them to save face with me during our conversations.

Create Targeted Questions

After undergoing the second phase, you should be able to come up with questions that will peg your clusters. *This* is the time to take your clusters into a controlled or lab environment and then see if you can recruit based on behavioral and motivation questions you have created.

This part of the screener usually has between three to five questions. We had one study where we only had to use one question—and the response allowed us to determine to which of four clusters a consumer belonged. You will need to ask other questions to see if they are a good candidate for the conversation, but these targeted questions could (should) really replace the standard ethnicity, age, gender, income, and life stage questions that are the cornerstone of most mass media/mass production work. I still include the standard demographic questions; however, I do so to help prove the point that these demographic markers are not important to the consumer's decision-making process. I always love it when we have one session with a 60-year-old female followed by a session with a 25-year-old male providing the same responses and reactions because they are part of the same cluster.

Once you have your participant in the room, you want to start with the same broad conversation you used before. You should be able to predict their answers and reaction to what you are going to show them at this point—even *before* you show it to them. This process provides powerful confirmation that your clusters are holding true.

Often, companies see these confirmation rounds as a wasted step. However, it's just as important to know that you have something right as it is to learn something new. You should view a clean study, in which you recruit people, predict how they will react, and send them on their way, positively, because it indicates that you are on the right track and ready to move forward with putting an artifact or experience out to a larger group. How do you know that you have learned something new? When you can do it with precision. Take advantage of the opportunity to watch consumers react to and adopt without having any issues with something you have built.

This is also a good time to consider going back to focus groups. Because you now know *why* you are putting a group of people in a room together, you can start using them in these defined clusters to do ideation or evaluate concepts. Make sure your recruiting questions truly address the clusters properly and form your groups around the clusters, not the demographics. A word of caution: pay attention to your clusters. Because some of them do not play nicely with one another, putting them in the same group might be a bad idea. Don't forget that their core behaviors and drivers will carry over to any research effort or initiative you attempt with the clusters.

Quantifying the Clusters

Once you have confirmed your clusters, you can now move to the stage of quantifying them. It's crucial to wait to take this step until you are confident that you're using the right questions—questions that recruit people accurately and put them in the right cluster. Your questions should be based on behaviors or attitudes; don't try to get your consumers to self-select into a cluster by defining it. Recall the cruise line example in Chapter 3. The question you would ask to put consumers into their cluster could be as simple as asking them to choose the statement that best matches them. For example:

- I primarily take a cruise to visit a new destination I have never visited before.
- I like the laid-back aspects of a cruise and enjoy spending time relaxing and being taken care of while on board.
- I cruise the same route every year with my friends because I enjoy hanging out with them and meeting new people.

Include a few more similar questions just to make sure there is no confusion. Then you can use these questions to divide and look at the sizes of your clusters.

The quantification step is great, because it's where you start to confirm some of the things you believe about your clusters—and learn additional knowledge about their overall ecosystem.

For example, let's say that you have a cluster that you know primarily relies on mainstream media for their news and information. You can confirm this hypothesis and start to identify their preferred mainstream channels for ad and product placement opportunities.

My best advice, however, is: don't get too hung up on quantification. This usually becomes the biggest stumbling block for a brand or company in our work with them. Laddering starts with *what you know*, so your existing quantification stands true. Laddering helps you understand more clearly how to target the clusters that have a propensity to be aligned to your company already and determine how to attract new groups.

Another important point to remember here is that size really doesn't matter. For example, you might have a small but influential cluster. In the old mass media world, it wouldn't make sense to target a group of that size. But as evidenced by the Pinterest story I shared in Chapter 2, one person can dramatically affect your brand or brand message.

There's a danger in ignoring some of your smaller groups, who most likely require a different level of interaction or authenticity to pique their interest. If you provide something to the masses merely because they are larger, but your brand is well aligned to this smaller group, you may completely miss out on the opportunity to reach them at all because of their refusal to participate in mass media. If this cluster sees something where everyone else sees it, then they will be unwilling to participate. It's not that they necessarily want exclusivity; they are simply motivated by the chance to try something out before others do. The opportunity to participate first and authentically with an experience or product is what really drives them. There's no notoriety necessary, and they will gladly spread your message for you. This cluster is just like the first domino in the series: you must knock it down first to get to the rest (Figure 5.1).

Figure 5.1 Understanding a Clusters Influence Is More Important Than Its Size

There is also the risk of performing what I call a *rinse and repeat.* I often talk with a marketing group, product group, or ad agency after a successful campaign and find that they're geared up for a repeat performance. Their plans will include sending an almost identical message to a group of people who successfully picked up their message or cause before. This completely misses the point, because they haven't taken the time to understand *why* it worked the first time. This is a dangerously expensive approach both in time and money, but it explains the proliferation of sequels and copycat programming we see in television, movies, advertising and other entertainment.

Listening to and Learning from the Clusters

The introduction of social media has made it easier than ever to watch your clusters in action—that is, of course, if they use social media. Social media can provide a more authentic and measurable reaction than almost any other research technique available for certain experiences; however, it has to be done correctly to reap these kinds of benefits.

You just need to reverse the way you listen. Instead of focusing on what is being said, focus on *who* is saying it. Again, it's not about the *what.* You can tell by the tone of the message (positive/ negative), the perspective (whether it's coming from I/you/we), and the information being shared via profiles how these groups are reacting to your campaigns or experiences. You will have a special insight into why they are speaking the way they are.

The Super Bowl provides an annual opportunity for you to easily separate your different clusters by viewing how they participate in the game. For instance, Chatty Cathys talk to other Chatty Cathys throughout the game primarily about the commercials. They use this unique opportunity to promote themselves and find interesting people to follow.

During an awards show, Passionate Penny will be glued to the Twitter feed or Facebook Fan page of her favorite actors, characters, or shows to experience the award show from that perspective. She will retweet or *like* a comment that highlights an accomplishment or receipt of an award. She will also be actively engaged on platforms from movie and television show databases such as IMDb or any other experience that provides her with additional content or exclusive information.

Granted, there are some groups whose members don't participate in social media at all. This is just as important; it lets you know where to put the best placement to reach them. Thanks to the research you've done, you know that you'll simply have to collect data from this group in a different way. It must take place in front of them, during their experience—not by trying to modify their behavior.

View every time you talk to a consumer in the future as an opportunity to test a concept or create an experience—to mark them into their defined cluster and to learn more about them. By doing so, you will begin to learn more and more about who they are and how they are going to react. By paying careful attention, you will learn when your clusters are changing or when there is a new marker that makes it important to potentially split them more granularly.

Thanks to this approach and continually learning, your consumers become almost as predictable as an old friend or one of your kids. You can forecast what they will say or do even before they do it. Don't make the mistake of viewing your conversations with consumers as a singular event.

Back in Chapter 3, I highlighted some work we did with the telephone company BellSouth. You might recall that we ended up with a panel for this project. Because we had recruited the panel members based on their core differences and motivations, we could predict and continue to learn from these consumers, even after that initial project was done. Without the ability to do this, the data we uncovered would have been confusing and nondirectional. Thanks to our background work and deep understanding of the different clusters, we had a relevant foundation from which we could work going forward.

The Importance of Transitional Clusters for Reach

I talked briefly about a cluster called Singular Sam in the previous chapter's study regarding social TV. You should never underestimate the importance of transitional clusters like this. Although Sam generally considers social media and television to be a waste of his time, there is one unique period of time during the year—his favorite sport's season—when he is not only willing but *excited* to participate in both. If you provide Singular Sam with something he considers valuable during this period (a Fantasy Football app, perhaps) and then add some elements that will hook him during a nontransitional time, you have the opportunity to establish a longer-term relationship with him outside of football season. You can therefore transition him from a singular user to a more permanent one.

For example, let's say Singular Sam is an Auburn fan and Auburn is having a great season. You can take this even further during the off-season if your station replays old Auburn games. This gives you the opportunity to promote to him within the Fantasy Football construct as a way to fill his precious TV time when football isn't on. Or perhaps you are an advertiser who knows that Singular Sam prefers in-person communication but uses a Fantasy Football application for the football season. This is a time when in-person ad placement, promotion, or partnership makes sense and achieves additional reach.

The great thing about laddering is that once you understand the factors that are important within the clusters—the DNA—you are able to find where the DNA overlaps. This knowledge allows you to create a *lattice*, just like the lattice you see on a trellis, that shows the overlap of groups and allows your brand, just like the branches of a rose bush growing across the trellis, to gain additional and solid reach. As we move into the next chapter, I will highlight what makes up the core *consumer DNA* of different clusters and discuss how to capitalize on their overlaps to really communicate with them.

Key Points

- Use a cross-functional team to do some blue-sky brainstorming and come up with concepts to test with your clusters.
- To confirm your clusters are accurate, you have to talk to the experts: the consumers.
- Once your clusters are strong, you can create simple questions that will identify your clusters in future studies.
- You can quantify the size of your clusters at the end of the process; however, it's something you should undertake with caution.
- Once you understand your clusters' behavior, you can create ways to listen to and learn from them. Use every opportunity to add to your knowledge.
- Identifying and understanding your transitional clusters will assist with gaining reach to more consumers.

The Social Media Family Case Study

Once I began analyzing how one can use social media across multiple industries and contexts, I realized that social media, unlike any other disruptive technology, is a manifestation of who we are at our core. We use it (or choose not to use it) as a way to express something about ourselves that goes well beyond what we choose to post, like, tweet, pin, or share.

This can be a difficult topic to explain to others. So in order to do so, I created a fictitious family that I call the TweetFaces. I am going to introduce you to this social media–loving family and give you an idea of what really makes them tick and why they do what they do.

It's important to understand that although the behaviors and motivations are all true in this example, gender, age, and other demographic components play no part in why these family members use social media the way they do. I have simply used likely representatives for each of them to make them more real.

TRADITIONAL TERRI

Let's start with grandma.

When you sign on to your Facebook wall, you probably see Terri's posts more than anyone else.

She loves Facebook. In fact, she uses it more than her kids do and will probably be using it long after everyone else has abandoned it. She has collected as many friends and family as possible—all the way back to her days in kindergarten.

However, Terri never posts anything original; instead, she typically shares something she has found on someone else's wall that she thinks is cute or even potentially shocking and untrue. She has no problem expressing her political opinions during election season and arguing about it with others via the comment stream. If chain letters still existed, Terri would be the one sending them along to others and making you feel guilty for breaking the chain.

Why Does She Share the Things She Shares?

The number one reason behind Terri's actions is that she wants you to remember her. She shares as an attempt to stay connected with those around her. You'll notice when you look closely at her posts that they are rarely about her. They're far more likely to be pictures of her grandkids, a breaking story she thinks everyone else must know about, or the latest "hilarious" cat video.

And although it may not initially appear so, you will see upon closer inspection that she carefully cultivates what she sends—and to whom. She is ultimately seeking some type of confirmation from her network of friends and family to assure her that they haven't forgotten her.

What is of Interest to Her?

Terri loves nostalgia: songs, people, and experiences that remind her of her past. She appreciates predictable humor, and although she can be a little edgy, she won't share anything that contains swear words or vulgarity (think PG-13-level humor). She is not the most technologically advanced; although she's recently adopted a smartphone, she uses only one or two applications on it (most likely Facebook for her phone and FaceTime) that primarily support her desire for connectivity to others. If technology doesn't support her longing for connection, she rarely has any use for it.

(continued)

(continued)

Terri wishes she could have her family around the dinner table at least once a week. However, she realizes that times have changed and that this isn't always possible, so she's willing to adapt to new ways of "getting together" in order to stay connected.

AMBITIOUS AMBER

Amber uses Facebook pretty regularly, especially to keep up with her friends from college. They are all at a stage where they are sharing information about their kids, what's going on in their lives, and where they went on their last vacation. She limits her network to her actual friends and family and rarely connects with people from work or other aspects of her life. To her, that's just creepy.

Amber is not interested in engaging in a Facebook battle with anyone else. She's very cautious about what she posts, especially during a political season or regarding divisive topics like religion.

She prefers to post things she has said, original content, not something canned or that she has found elsewhere. If she does post something she finds, she wants to be able to add her own twist; it won't just be something others have already posted or stated. She likes to think she finds new things, but she's really capitalizing on something someone else has found for her.

Amber uses Twitter but primarily for getting news. She follows a few celebrities but that's not her primary driver for its use. However, Amber absolutely loves Pinterest. She can keep up with her favorite things and organize them in a visual way. She probably uses Pinterest more now than any other network. Although she's not sure she would call it social, it does give her an idea about what's going on in other's lives and gives her a place to dream.

Why Does She Share the Things She Shares?

Amber wants others to perceive her as being successful. She wants people to think that she has her life together and that her family is doing well. She protects her public persona very carefully.

She cares a lot about what people think about her—but not, she thinks, in a needy way. She's merely concerned with keeping up appearances. She is establishing herself in the world and therefore wants to appear professional. She knows that everything she puts out into social media could help or hurt her in the future, because it's going to be there forever.

What is of Interest to Her?

Amber enjoys smart humor, something that is current and unpredictable. She loves to be the first (or think that she is the first) to share new ideas, trends, recipes, or links. She relies on pop culture and mass media outlets to get her news and to develop an understanding of the world around her.

She loves her iPad and smartphone. She feels that they keep her connected to the world while she is on the go or sitting on the couch snuggled up next to her husband.

EVERYMAN EDDIE

Eddie is married to Amber and has a limited interest in social media and technology—but in general, he doesn't get the

(continued)

(continued)

appeal. He believes that people share too much and that social media sites pose a privacy risk. He also thinks that technology should support your life, not be the center of it, and that many people use it as a substitution for or way to avoid real life.

Eddie prefers to have conversations with others in person. He talks about all the same topics that others discuss via social media—funny commercials, videos, sports, or other current events—while hanging out with his close buddies. He's been friends with these people since high school and college and feels lucky that he still lives close enough to most of them to catch a game, play golf, or meet up for happy hour after work.

Eddie only has a few friends within social media, a total somewhere between 10 and 25. He pays attention to Facebook when Amber points something out, when there is something going on with someone very close to him (a new baby in a friend's family, for example), or if others are discussing a topic he cares about, such as sports or hot news. But other than that, he usually stays off these sites.

Eddie recently traded in his flip phone for a smartphone. The only reason he did it was because he felt that he needed to learn to text to stay connected with his teenage daughters. He also realized and there were a couple of applications that could help him out with his golf game.

Why Does He Share the Things He Shares?

The fact is that Eddie rarely shares. His refusal to use social media is a silent plea for times gone by when people gathered and spent time together in person. Although he might *like* someone's posts, he will rarely respond to a post another person makes on his wall. He is most likely to share something he learned online while talking with his friends offline. However, he does watch streaming video of news stories or the big game if he can't catch them on television in real time.

What is of Interest to Him?

Eddie is the great lurker. He uses social media to keep up with what his close friends and especially his family are doing. He does use technology to have conversations with his friends about his favorite sports teams, but he does so via private methods such as text messages or e-mail. He doesn't see the appeal in sharing his opinions in the open, and because he likes to trash talk a bit, he worries he might offend others who don't understand. Any application that gives him access to more information about his favorite team or sport is appealing.

VICE VICKY

Vicky is Eddie and Amber's oldest daughter. She was living on her own but had to move back into her parents' house when her roommate split. Her job at the local coffee shop is enough to let her pay her bills and have some fun but not enough for her to live on her own. She takes the occasional class at the local technical college and hopes to be a paralegal or work at the front desk of a doctor's office.

Vicky wants to appear independent and edgy. She wants what she says, wears, and even does to have an element of shock value. She has no problem associating herself with vice brands—Skyy Vodka, Marlboro cigarettes, Jack Daniels Whiskey, for example—on social media and often talks about alcohol or the clubs where she and her friends hang out.

(continued)

(*continued*)

She uses Facebook to keep up with some friends but loves the instant and short bursts of banter she can create on Twitter. She is a friend collector and needs to meet a person only once or communicate with them via social media to add them to her pool.

She often uses her personal brand and network of friends to promote her favorite new band or club. Vicky wouldn't admit it out loud, but it's very important that others respond to what she posts. She will even take a post down if it doesn't garner the response she expected.

She is turned off by goofy humor and looks for what she would call authentic comedy. She loves reality shows like *Keeping Up with the Kardashians* and was very sad when MTV cancelled *Jersey Shore*.

Why Does She Share the Things She Shares?

Vicky shares mainly to have other people notice her. She wants/craves the attention that comes with being different. She doesn't care if what she shares is offensive; in fact, her exact intention is often to stir something up. She stays away from mainstream pop culture because she is too cool for that. She loves to talk about her favorite reality shows, especially those that involve high drama between the main characters.

What is of Interest to Her?

Vicky is interested in vice brands or activities: alcohol, cigarettes, clubs, tattoos, piercings, and alternative, edgy bands. She likes crude humor, especially humor at others' expense, or anything that lets her look like she is better than someone else. She uses Twitter because she thinks it makes her cooler but hasn't abandoned Facebook and doesn't see the draw of Pinterest.

COOL CADE

Cade is Vicky's on-again, off-again boyfriend.

He is naturally curious and constantly seeking a new experience. It's not enough for him to see others doing something; Cade wants to try it for himself. He also likes trying new technology or products before everyone else. It's important to him that he adopt these devices after finding them on his own through an obscure blog or StumbleUpon (a website that allows users to stumble upon new information by following tags) not because someone else told him about it.

He likes things to be a little difficult or unique but not overly complex. He knows and watches shows such as *Lost* and *Mad Men* before anyone else. But once others start watching a show and it becomes popular, Cade moves on and begins looking for the next obscure show.

Cade primarily uses Twitter and Google+; Facebook is of lesser concern to him. He uses it mainly to keep in touch with a close group of friends. Yes, he has been to the DragonCon conference with his friends that are into comic books and superheroes; he didn't dress up, but some of the friends in his circle did.

Why Does He Share the Things He Shares?

Cade shares very quietly. He might see something new and buy it, but he won't tell others about it unless they ask or he will tweet a picture without much explanation. He is equally balanced between interaction online and in person. He expects technology to enhance his experiences in life, not replace them.

(continued)

(continued)

What Is of Interest to Him?

Anything new, different, or unique appeals to Cade. He craves knowing what's next but doesn't want anyone to tell him this; he wants to find it on his own. Cade is the most connected of all people but represents one of the smallest clusters. He enjoys meeting new and diverse groups of people.

Careful Callie

Amber and Eddie's younger daughter has just started high school.

If asked, Callie will say that she is very careful about what she shares, but in reality, she tends to share too much about her feelings. She might post something about how badly her day is going or that she just broke up with her boyfriend.

Callie knows that both her parents and her friends are using social media to watch and judge her, so she keeps her content PG-13. She occasionally shares or says something that she feels is shocking. It's usually not as scandalous as anything her sister Vicky posts, but Callie feels as though she has crossed the line.

Callie craves interaction from others, not just a confirmation or a like from them. She is disappointed if she posts something to her wall and no one responds—and like her sister, she may actually take the post down if this happens. In addition, Callie's posts usually start with "I." She talks about herself, what's going on her life, how her day was, or that studying for her test is just too hard.

She has lots of friends on Facebook and is not above starting and engaging in a Facebook war on various topics. Callie rarely uses Twitter and enjoys sharing pictures of her animals and clothing on Instagram.

Why Does She Share the Things She Shares?

Callie's primary motivation is a desire for attention. She needs affirmation from others and uses social media as a way to enhance her self-esteem. She is more likely to share when a friend encourages her or assures her that what she is sharing is interesting or okay. She's also more likely to post a funny video or picture that she sees others sharing than to comment within another feed because she wants the credit for having found it.

What Is of Interest to Her?

Callie prefers messages that let her talk about herself—how she is feeling and what's going on with her. She keeps up with more mainstream pop culture like *American Idol*, *The Voice*, or the new *Hunger Games* movie and what's going on with pop/country singer Taylor Swift. She likes more juvenile, safe humor and would never intentionally hurt someone else's feelings or make fun of them, even though her comments sometimes come across that way.

Now that you have met the TweetFaces, you will recognize the *why* behind their social media use much more readily. Of course, this is not an exhaustive list of social media clusters, and there are certainly groups that do not participate in social media at all. Their why for not participating is as important and interesting as understanding the why of those who do participate. Understanding your consumers' why is the first step toward building products, services, and experiences in a way that is meaningful to them.

6

Latticing

Finding the Overlap in Ladders

Deep inside us we're not that different at all.

—Phil Collins

THE FOLLOWING BLOG post was written by Nicole Ovens, one of my colleagues at User Insight, in September 2012. It talks specifically about how social media has helped bridge the gap between individuals. It also supports the notion that we are driven by experiences and issues at our core and looks at how different forces of nurture and nature affect the way we live our lives.

It is just as important to look for these types of intersections, understand why they exist within your consumer groups, and assess how the different clusters interact and act at these intersections as it is to understand each individual cluster's laddering. This post sums up the difference this latest round of disruptive technology has made to our lives:

We live in an amazing time—one during which social networking has brought attention to health issues that were [once] considered too insignificant to study. [Today's online interaction has] provided support for those of us who once thought, "Wow, I am so different from everyone else I know." This digital revolution increased awareness and identified a hidden demand surrounding a health issue that is near and dear to my life.

Thirty years ago, I was diagnosed with celiac disease. It took almost seven years (most of my life, to that point) to discover what was wrong with me. Misdiagnosis after misdiagnosis and invasive test after invasive test and finally . . . the silver bullet: all you have to do is stop eating wheat. Well—wheat, barley, oats, rye, and alfalfa sprouts. That was the advice of the time; [and though it was] simple advice, [it] certainly was not easy.

Back in the early 80s, I had to live with my "special diet." I also had to say goodbye to my two favorite foods: pizza and Wheat Thins. My mom did her best by making crumbly, bland

119

birthday cakes and packing rice cake and peanut butter (sometimes ham) sandwiches for lunch.

I know correlation doesn't mean causation, but it's not a coincidence that life began improving big time right here in the United States starting in 2007. You may ask how I can pinpoint 2007 with such confidence. I can, because, I went to Italy in the fall of 2006. In Italy, every corner *farmacia* had a gluten-free section and sold over-the-counter "Xeliac" home tests. When in Rome, I learned that all Italian children are screened for celiac. I remember asking myself (and others) why was it that in Italy—where pasta and pizza reign—that people are so aware of celiac disease. I can remember expecting to get ill when I planned that trip—but I never did. I felt great the whole time, because I never once had a meal that was accidentally cross-contaminated with wheat. I also never felt like I didn't have enough choice, such that I chose to take a risk. I remember coming back home, wishing the United States was so celiac-friendly. It didn't take long before that simple wish came true.

The very next year, I started hearing that some restaurants in nearby Knoxville [were offering] gluten-free menu items. Then, in 2008, two restaurants in my tiny town of Oak Ridge also opened catering to people with gluten intolerance. Another red-letter day in 2008 happened when Chex cereal, a mainstream brand, started advertising that Rice Chex and Corn Chex were now gluten-free. Prior to all of this the only major brand I remember being so consumer-friendly was Disney— "where all little girl's wishes come true."

So what happened to launch this great transformation in 2007? Social networking went mainstream, and took the digital revolution to a whole new level. Online tools proliferated, giving consumers better access to information and an easy way to build communities that broke down geographic barriers and accommodated our busy lifestyles. All of a sudden, patients and parents dealing with hundreds of issues like celiac disease could join virtual support communities, share advice, recommend doctors, and link to news stories and websites with disease information.

Although it's told from one person's point of view, there are many players in the story above. And even though each one is participating in different ways and for different reasons, they are all participating in an authentic relationship. Yes, the restaurants and products are making money addressing this need, but they're doing so based on an awareness of a niche need that they've chosen to address. Mayo Clinic researchers estimate that the number of people suffering from celiac disease is about 1 in every 100. Although 1 percent might not seem like enough to warrant a response, it has. In this era of mass customization, addressing this need for those affected and tapping into the goodwill of those who care about them is appropriate and important.

Once you have undergone the laddering exercise and understand what drives each of your individual clusters, you can then take the time to lattice your customer groups. This step will help you identify where they do and don't overlap, where to focus your efforts, and which initiatives will have the greatest impact. It lets you determine the common starting point for the clusters you seek to reach.

Take into Account Standard Demographics

All of my analysis uses something to indicate a group's demographic markers, just to see if a pattern exists. Most of the time, the research simply uncovers a propensity for a group to be slightly more male or female. I would say that the split is often more 50/50 on certain markers, our societal norms cause either the male or the female to suppress core tendencies for some of the *consumer DNA* I have uncovered. For example, one DNA marker is the propensity to *project*, to let others know about your feelings or emotions. Men have traditionally been raised to learn *not* to do this. But recent disruptive technology, social media in particular, allows the male who wants to project to do so and to do it without fear of judgment.

Pop culture, digital technology, and entertainment expert Johanna Blakley made this argument in her 2011 TED Talk (www.youtube.com/watch?v=ZR4LdnFGzPk). Blakley spoke specifically about how social media is "the end of gender," how it allows us to escape the boxes that we've been putting ourselves and others in. She argues that shared interests and values are more important than standard demographics.

Once you have laddered your consumers, you get beneath even the most superficial categories of interest and values to an understanding of *why*. And this is always the crucial question to ask because it allows you to speak to your consumers in a language that is basic to their underlying drivers. Why does a group participate in an interest or have a shared value? What are they trying to accomplish? What is their goal? Are they seeking a connection or correction to something in their past? Are they trying to prevent something in the future? Is it based on expectations or failures from their past?

Applying a layer of standard demographic information as an overlay helps us understand how life circumstances affect a group's core. For instance, having less or more money might compel a spender to allocate his or her money in different ways. It doesn't change that person's core DNA of having a tendency to spend; it just changes the mechanisms of spending and perhaps the items purchased.

Common Consumer DNA

There are several factors that comprise the chains of *consumer DNA* that I commonly encounter. I call it *consumer DNA* because it's the building blocks on which I start to evaluate and determine how the user groups relate to one another.

One of the best things about my work at User Insight is the fact that it has allowed me to focus on becoming a specialist on the end user, or the consumer. When I first started the company, clients often asked if our company specialized in a single industry or concentrated on one type of technology or product offering. Because the company was established and has grown during an incredibly disruptive time, if it had been that narrowly focused, it wouldn't be in business today. The one mantra, the one unbroken rule that I am sure to follow, is that I *always talk to users*. I never assume anything about the consumer, and I always pay attention to and advocate for the user's needs, expectations, and desires.

This approach means that my knowledge is several miles wide and several feet deep, which gives me the unique perspective to see if and how clusters map across industries and experiences. And amazingly, I've found that they do. The crucial types of factors are consistently the same; they just show up in different sequence for different contexts.

This *consumer DNA* is what makes the difference in how you communicate with and between different clusters, and they include:

Marker A	Marker B	Difference between Markers
Know—Is truly educated about a topic or subject thanks to firsthand experience or knowledge.	*Doesn't Know*—Doesn't have firsthand knowledge; relies instead on others to provide the evidence needed to make a decision or judgment.	This is one of the more difficult factors to determine. If a person falls in the category of *doesn't know* and *project*, then that person will share things with others without having firsthand knowledge. This combination of DNA makes the person want to be the first to tell others about new discoveries or information—he or she wants to appear to be the one who knows. However, it's crucial in this case to understand the true source of the knowledge. Did the consumer actually find the information firsthand?
Project—Openly shares aspects of his or her life via social media channels or in person.	*Doesn't Project*—Typically takes a backseat; shares only when asked or to affirm others.	Does the person tell others about the details of his or her life openly, or is the person more reserved? A powerful combination I see in *consumer DNA* is the group that *knows* and *doesn't project*. Others listen when they share, because it's so rare and out of character for them. The way they share is also very unique; they may simply do so by taking a picture, posting it, and doing nothing more.
Willing to Change—Is often seeking change; wants to try the new, untested technologies or experiences.	*Not Willing to Change*—Has a mantra something like, "If it's not broken, why mess with it?" Will not move to a new technology or experience easily without prodding.	Is the person open to change? Will the person make accommodations for technology or process in his or her life, or does the person expect the technology to meet his or her needs? Recall from Chapter 4's case study that Showless Joe is not willing to change during the regular TV viewing season, but as Singular Sam, he will change to participate in Fantasy Football with his friends.

124

Marker A	Marker B	Difference between Markers
Cares about Other's Opinion—Very careful about what is posted and where; may look for approval from others before posting.	*Doesn't Care about Other's Opinion*—Will say anything to anyone—either on social media or in person—without really considering the long-term impact of words or actions.	Is this person concerned about what others think about what is shared? Does this person conform to external influences about how he or she should dress and act, or is this person content to marching to his or her own drum? Vice Vicky from Chapter 5's social media family fits into the second category here. She is fine with using salty language and doesn't seem to acknowledge the impact her current actions will have on her future self.
Expects Authentic—Must have experiences that are real and as close to true as possible; enjoys spending time off the beaten path.	*Okay with Artificial*—Likes things to be predictable or a known quantity. Prefers to go safe places, for example, Disney World or a tourist attraction.	Consumers that crave authenticity must have the experience firsthand. They can't be told that something is good or simply read a review. If it's food, they will go to the restaurant to get a taste before talking about it. If it's art, they must see the actual painting before offering an opinion. On the other hand, people who are okay with artificial are content visiting the same places all the other tourists do and are actually *more* comfortable with a known experience.

(continued)

125

(continued)

Marker A	Marker B	Difference between Markers
Heavily Invested—Is willing to work hard for an end result.	*Less Invested*—Is seeking the path of least resistance; wants whatever it is to work with as little effort as possible.	This component of the *consumer DNA* is most likely to change based on the context. Are they willing to go the extra mile to try something out? Or do they give up if the task at hand turns out to be more difficult than expected? If these consumers are very interested in the topic—perhaps their favorite sport or saving money—they'll likely be willing to spend more time trying to accomplish the task. If it's something they could care less about, they will move on quickly (especially if it's difficult to do.)
Online—Is more comfortable connecting, maintaining, and nurturing relationships using technology.	*In Person*—Prefers to spend time with people physically, at a local hangout or a common meeting place.	Is the individual's idea of interaction more focused around meeting people in person, or is the person more comfortable using technology and social media to stay in touch? The division between a preference for online and offline is a significant DNA marker I see in studies. You must know where your consumer prefers to relate to you. This is especially important to uncover because it is a preference that you cannot change.
Has or Seeks Friends Who Are Like Them—Collects or communicates with others who are like them: others who go to their same church, belong to the same clubs, or have the same political affiliation, for example.	Has or Seeks Friends Who Are Not Like Them—Is more interested in meeting new people who come from a differing background or experience.	This DNA marker speaks to the consumer's acceptance of new things, experiences, and openness to adventure. Who this individual chooses to associate with and seek out as friends is a good indicator of how safe he or she wishes to play it.

126

This is by no means an exhaustive list of the different factors that can appear in *consumer DNA*. However, it does represent some strong patterns I have seen across projects. The factors that are on or off may vary in different contexts, even for the same consumer. You will also notice that none of these markers include items such as money, life stage, or gender. Consumers develop some of these markers as part of their nature (things that have been true about them since they were born) and as part of their nurture (how they were raised and the circumstances they faced throughout their lives).

You can use the major factors that you determine exist within your clusters to start looking for overlap. If you manage multiple brands or experiences within your portfolio, you should analyze the important DNA according to those discrete brands or experiences. You can't assume the DNA is the same if the brands within your portfolio are different. I will discuss the concept of *lensing* in more detail in the next chapter. This includes analyzing how people from the outside world truly perceive your brand, which gives you an idea of the attributes that are most important to mapping your clusters. This allows you to build the construct cleanly, without a prejudice toward a brand, experience, or discrete choices. The objective is to understand your consumers for who they are, where they are, and why.

For now, just remember the way that different groups relate to one another is never the same from one context or interaction to the next. You can't rely on a template or standard construct to present every relationship between groups. It's crucial that you choose a construct that allows you to explain *all* of your users within that framework.

Look for Overlap

We all have DNA that overlaps, and laddering works the same way. Once you establish a core understanding of your user groups, you start to recognize which elements are the same between the different clusters. They just won't be the demographic markers you are used to looking at and using. Instead of paying attention to whether or not a person is male or female, you will look at differences such as, "Does this person project or not?" And, "Is this person interested in authentic experiences, or does he or she like predictability?"

The step of latticing takes a page directly out of the old segmentation or demographic playbook; however, instead of focusing on the attributes that are easily recognizable and part of that old approach—age, sex, gender, income, education, amount of spend, and number of visits—and then looking for patterns, you assess the data you have about your clusters based on their *consumer DNA*.

Does your consumer cluster care about authentic experiences? If so, your marketing efforts, product, and brand must support their desire to experience things in real life. They must taste, touch, hold, and see whatever you offer for themselves. A digital experience alone isn't likely to be enough.

Does your consumer cluster need affirmation? If this is the case, make sure your marketing and social media campaigns include a way to acknowledge consumers, especially if they interact with your brand. If you ignore a group that needs affirmation, you're almost guaranteed to lose them as brand, service, or product champions.

These markers become the new framework by which you can create products, services, and marketing messages and even determine how to provide support.

Analyzing overlap is important because it allows you to understand which group(s) to target for a certain product, service, campaign, or experience. It also shows you how various groups influence and interact with one another—in other words, what their ecosystem is. Yes, the ultimate goal is to get your message out to the right person. The thought and associated activities behind rolling out a new idea, brand, or concept is far more important, strategic, and complex than in years past. Latticing your user groups and looking for overlap, developing something that I call a *lattice construct*, tells

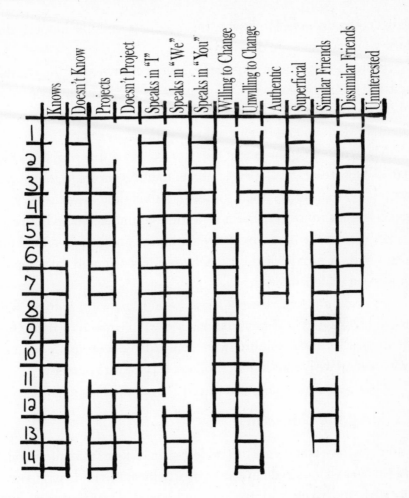

Figure 6.1   Lattice Construct

you how and where to target for the greatest impact. The added bonus of a *lattice construct* is it can be used to create a timeline and approach for reaching the other groups (see Figure 6.1).

Thankfully, you don't need the same level of background I have to successfully ladder your consumer groups. You need only to follow this book's instructions: start by having broad conversations with your consumers, in their environment. Dive deeper to understand your consumers within the context of your industry or focus. You should know your consumers as well as you understand how your company works, how your products are developed, and how your messages are distributed.

Build your product, experience, service, or marketing strategy starting from who your consumers are at their core by developing an understanding of their DNA and accepting that you cannot change them. Rather, you must conform to them.

My experience has taught me over the years that very few companies view their development and marketing efforts in the correct way. It's far easier for them to assume that they know their consumer groups than to spend a little time to understand what really makes them tick—and why. Very few bother and merely try to build a generalized profile of their ideal consumer through sales reports or a broad understanding.

By spending some time—*any time*—talking with your consumers and seeking to understand them, you will be much further ahead than most in understanding what really drives consumers in their relationship with your brand, product, service, or company.

Building the Construct

After you have completed the laddering techniques that allow you to understand your individual users, you will instinctively begin to identify what underlying patterns exist and how these patterns define the difference between the groups. At this point, you should test your instinct and include others to help defend or deny your assumptions.

I call this part of the project a war room. Start by hanging all the pictures of the consumers to whom you have spoken on the walls with a bulleted breakdown of what you know about them. Then, begin trying to match them to one another. What makes them the same? What makes them vastly different? How can you explain them succinctly to others outside of the room who have not participated in the laddering exercises? I use all the standard constructs you are probably used to seeing from consulting firms: Venn diagrams, x/y axis charts, and scatterplots. But sometimes I need to depict a very unique relationship. For example, I affectionately called one of our drawings the batwing because it looked like the symbol that Gotham city uses to summon its masked hero.

The visualization process forces you to really think through what you know. I will sometimes attempt an early version during the laddering process between the initial round of laddering and the confirmation round. This helps in beginning to identify the critical factors, may point to additional information I need to pick up, or highlights parts of the laddering process that are not as important within the context.

Recall the bank study I cited in Chapter 2 regarding the word *convenience*. I was convinced that money was a factor for this project; after all, I was talking with consumers about where they kept their money. But one of my team members disagreed with me and felt that it wasn't a driver. I realized that it didn't make sense to apply money as a factor during my attempts to do so in the war room session, so I dropped it. It wasn't until I tried to explain how the consumer groups latticed that I was able to clearly see it as an unimportant factor even though it was a common theme in the laddering conversations.

Can a Consumer Move between Clusters?

A cluster can't live in two places. So if your construct is telling you that they do, then something isn't right, either with your construct or potentially your context (for instance, it may not be narrow enough). You need to be able to explain how, if ever, a consumer moves from one part of the construct to another.

Identifying how and when a consumer moves from one part of the lattice to another is as important as identifying the different groups. This is the most powerful place to intercept a consumer: when that person is in transit. If the consumer is using a competitor's product, you can convert this person by providing evidence that you will do a better job of meeting his or her needs while they are transitioning.

This is where models like Groupon often fail. Groupon, and other companies, try to convert consumers to new constructs by offering discounted versions of their product, service, or experience. These types of deals speak to one part of the consumer's DNA, a desire to get a deal or save money, but they are not targeted to the right *consumer DNA* groups for the brand. Another mistake merchants make is treating those consumers who use the Groupon deal differently than their regular customers. Groupon users can see through this smoke screen; they know that the deal is a temporary change to the brand, not a conscious decision on the brand's part to move within this new consumer's core DNA driver. It's therefore very unlikely that this person will become a new, permanent customer once the deal is done, unless something speaks to his or her core DNA during the experience with the merchant. The consumer sees the execution for what it is: different than what is normally done or delivered. There is rarely a long-term benefit to either party.

We often see a similar phenomenon in our laddering work, called the try it once, never again factor. This explains the success of a gimmick or the concept of viral videos. People want to participate in the trend or the greater conversation when it comes to something that is having its 15 minutes of fame, but it's not about developing an additional relationship with new consumers. In fact, just like Chatty Cathy, consumers use these types of gimmicks to satisfy something in their core DNA. These stunts are good for temporary uplift; they don't go very far in terms of encouraging long-term consumer loyalty from the groups that naturally identify with the brand or company attributes. Most of the time, consumers merely remember the video and not the product or brand being advertised.

Using the Lattice for Better Measurement

Latticing not only helps you identify your opportunities for the next new initiative; it also narrows your focus on what is important to *measure.* You can use the lattice to unlock your big data and make it actionable and useful beyond being just a collection of information on different groups.

For instance, let's say that you discover that a cluster's DNA includes a particular strand. In this case, it's a tendency for them to share how they feel. This group is connected with another cluster that will comment only on what the first cluster shares; however, the second cluster will not share anything themselves. You can measure a campaign or product experience's success by monitoring the interactions between these two groups. In other words, it's not about unique likes, shares, or offline conversations; it's also about others' reactions to those occurrences, within their own DNA tendencies and behaviors. It's crucial to view success by measuring it from the consumer's perspective.

Different groups' core *consumer DNA* lets you define the behaviors you would expect to see (or not see) from each. If the cluster is willing to change and likes to project, a technology or experience that supports these preferences and desires, such as the features in Foursquare that allow people to check in to a location and tell others about their experience, will work well. Conversely, this technology will fail miserably with groups that are unwilling to change even if they like to project.

It's at this point in the process that you can begin to look at your brand, company, experience, or marketing message. Regrettably, this is where most companies start: by talking and thinking about themselves and their brands. By waiting to start this evaluation process until you can view your company, brand, or product through your end user's perspective, you really learn how to make a difference in how you reach and communicate with your end consumers.

The next chapter explains lensing exercises, a process that helps you identify where you currently stand with your consumers. It's a valuable way to evaluate everything you consider doing from your consumer clusters' perspective and it is the most powerful and rewarding part of the consumer-focused laddering process—the payoff for all your work.

Key Points

- Use standard demographic markers to filter what you have identified in your clusters, but only to understand if a certain marker has a higher likelihood to map to a given demographic.
- There is a common set of *consumer DNA*, the markers that define an individual and separate clusters into their individual groups.
- By identifying the overlapping DNA markers between clusters, you can understand how your clusters are different and similar.
- Building a *lattice construct* clarifies these overlaps, gives you a model for explaining them to others, and pinpoints what causes a cluster to move from one part of the construct to another.
- The lattice construct provides valuable insight into unlocking the data you are collecting by providing you with a way to view how the clusters relate to one another and to identify what is truly important to each of the clusters within a context.
- Consumers can and do move between clusters within the construct. This movement is the most powerful time to capture and convert them because they are outside of their core DNA, giving you an opportunity to build something in this transition that will capture them once they return to their core.

Travel Personas Case Study

One task that technological disruptions have had a dramatic impact on in recent years is making travel plans. Internet booking engines such as Expedia, Travelocity, Kayak, and Hotels.com have revolutionized travel by giving consumers the power to easily gather information from across the Internet and compare prices. Travelers no longer have to depend on a travel agent to make their travel decisions.

These consolidated search sites leveled the playing field and empowered travelers to book their own travel because it gave them access to the same level of information that was previously available only to the experts. Today, the tools available to the average consumer are often even better—and the knowledge richer—than that on most experts' systems. Combine that with the fact that consumers know themselves better than the travel agent does and it's no surprise that the travel industry was completely up-ended.

We recognized a trend within the travel sites: most of them focus largely on price. However, as I discussed earlier in the book, we know that money is not really the core driver in making decisions. So then what *does* compel people to choose to travel somewhere? We undertook a laddering project to understand how travelers were clustering based on this disruption.

We learned a universal truth: all travelers incorporate some type of aggregator site into their research behavior when booking hotels or airlines. However, these sites have very little influence on what airline they fly, where they stay, or the all-important *why* behind their travel choices.

We started our laddering exercises in the travel space by asking consumers broad questions about their favorite activities and what they do in their free time, where, and with whom. We

(continued)

(*continued*)

wanted to get a feel for the influencers and the way these consumers talk about and interact with others in their day-to-day life. We knew this would provide clues about their core *consumer DNA*.

We then narrowed the scope, asking consumers to describe their ideal vacation; in particular, we wanted to understand what elements would make it ideal and what they valued most about their free time.

We continued to draw consumers closer to our true goal by asking them about actions they were going to take toward their next vacation—what they were going to do and why—in an attempt to figure out how they would plan this trip. We knew we could uncover information about their true behavior by giving them a concrete problem to work on, but we also knew that we could keep the scope wider by doing this than we might if we simply asked, "What sites would you use?"

The lead-up questions garnered unexpected knowledge. It also kept the consumer from figuring out the game, because at this point, we could be talking about *any* aspect of the travel experience.

We began to see patterns emerge as we asked these questions. The more we talked with consumers, the more their answers started to sound just like someone else's and clusters started to form around the distinct differences in vacation habits.

The following are the clusters of primary drivers or differentiators that had an impact on their decision:

- There is a group that just wants to *relax*. These consumers wanted to park on a beach and do nothing—make no plans and have no responsibilities.
- Another group of people were traveling to *visit friends and family*. They usually picked places to visit based on whether they knew someone there, and many had a contact list of

friends who lived all over the world. They were really good at keeping in touch with people.

- A third cluster was all about seeking *adventure* and never wanted to visit the same place twice. They usually wanted to go somewhere unusual and participate in an authentic or local experience while there.
- The last group was interested in *history*. They gravitate toward locales with historical significance, want to learn everything there is to know about the places they visited, and had a list of must-sees from previous vacations.

Now that we know what the various clusters are seeking, let's revisit our original goal: to figure out what the ideal travel website should look like. The travel cluster type is a crossroads as represented in Figure 6.2.

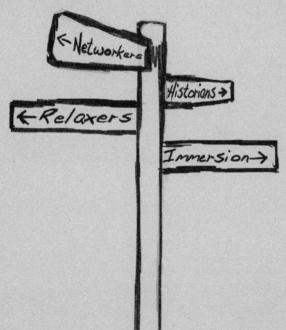

Figure 6.2 There Are Four Drivers for the Broad Topic of Travel

(continued)

(continued)

We named the group that wanted to visit friends and family the networkers. The group that wanted to sit on a beach and do nothing was dubbed relaxers. The all-about-adventure group was the immersion seekers, and the group that wanted to know everything about places they visited was (naturally) named the historians.

Those became the major drivers: people, destination, planning, and culture. Some people go on vacation to get away, whereas others do it to get together. Some want an exotic destination, and others crave something familiar. Some people are planners, whereas others live on spontaneity. Some people want to live like the locals; some just want to observe them. The drivers in this case, while similar to the cruise line study are broader because the context is broader and choices wider. Let's look at the four clusters more closely.

NETWORKER NANCY

Let me introduce you to our networker, Nancy. Although she seeks adventure, she's always surrounded by friends or family, so people are her primary driver. She wants to experience the local culture from the point of view of her friends. She uses social networks as a way to keep in touch with everyone, but she probably keeps some form of an address book as well.

Features that we would build into a website for Nancy might include a trip tracker or some way to publish where she's going and where she's been as a way to help her bring people together. A site that recently piqued Nancy's interest is Startup Stay. This tool lets her find fellow business owners in other markets who she can stay with and people with whom she can connect when they visit her hometown.

We notice certain trends about Nancy. She wants to be with people; the destination isn't as important to her; she's happy to see the culture from her contact's point of view. We know that her major driver is people, and it's part of her core *consumer DNA* to be friends with people who are not like her.

RELAXER RONALD

Ronald is a relaxer. He has a family and is interested in doing the exact opposite of his home life when he's on vacation; that is, he simply wants to kick back and totally relax. One of Ronald's major drivers is spontaneity. He doesn't have time to plan anything, so he's not going to research his trip very heavily.

Ronald is likely to vacation at the same place every year, even going so far as staying in the same condo. Unlike Nancy, he wants to spend time with people like him. The idea of all-inclusive vacation is appealing to him, because it takes away any requirement for him to think.

IMMERSION EDNA

Next up is Edna, an immersion seeker. She doesn't like planning, but she knows that it's necessary to make sure she gets an authentic experience. Edna hates doing touristy things and would never visit the same place twice. She wants to immerse herself in every aspect of the trip: language, culture, and food.

Edna is interested in *experience* rather than observation; she wants to know where to be rather than what to see. She also wants to know specific details about a location so that she can come prepared. Edna is all about the extremes: she wants to be

(continued)

(continued)

away from people she knows, in an exotic destination, enjoying an authentic cultural experience—and contrary to how it would seem, she has to follow a schedule so that she's prepared.

Edna is very interested in authentic experience. She doesn't want to take pictures of the Eiffel Tower. She'd rather be muddling her way through a failed attempt at ordering in French at some backstreet cafe no one has ever heard of before, a place she found using her smartphone application 5 minutes before she decided she wanted to eat.

HISTORIAN HELEN

Finally, there's Helen. She represents our last group: the historians. Helen seeks locations with a sense of history and culture and likes a combination of relaxation and adventure. For example, she would be okay with a day or two on the beach doing nothing. But after a while, she would get bored and want to partake in some kind of planned activity, such as a tour of the area.

Helen does her homework before a trip and picks out some things to do, because she wants to explore culture through historical locations. She is interested in gathering maps of the area or getting recommendations on must-see attractions. Helen wants to go to a location and to see all the sights that are outlined for her, those that are on her bucket list.

One additional group we uncovered is a group we call the compromise group. This is a set of individuals who let someone else take the lead when it comes to travel. They don't have a strong desire for travel one way or the other. In fact, they would be just as happy having a staycation (spending time at home versus traveling somewhere) as they would be actually going somewhere. This group can transition to one of the other categories by being introduced to an experience that resonates with their core—or by potentially even being introduced to travel for the first time. This group will mention other people in their conversations about travel and travel plans. They are never the person who puts the trip together; they are truly just along for the ride.

You can see how truly different each cluster is as you consider them together. Although there is overlap, the primary drivers are what push people one way or another. It would be a mistake to treat all of these clusters the same way, as many of the aggregator sites do today. It's far better to use their behaviors as a driver to take them to experiences, information, and applications that match their primary reasons for traveling.

7

Lensing

Imagination is not only the uniquely human capacity to envision that which is not, and therefore the fount of all invention and innovation. In its arguably most transformative and revelatory capacity, it is the power that enables us to empathize with humans whose experiences we have never shared.

—J.K. Rowling

ON THE TV screen, a red convertible whips by a man walking along the side of the road. The car stops and reverses back to the man, presumably to ask him if he needs a ride. The beautiful woman driving the convertible rolls down the window, lowers her sunglasses so you can see her eyes, and asks the man seductively, "Are those Levi's jeans you are wearing?"

What red-blooded American male *wouldn't* run out and buy a pair of Levi's jeans after seeing that commercial? Equally, what woman wouldn't envision herself as the main character in that ad—in control, asking the questions, treating the man as the sex object?

One of the major tenets of advertising has traditionally been an attempt to make consumers see themselves using the product and replacing the image of the person on the screen with themselves. The goal was to drive demand for the product through the influence of suggestion or role-play, with the marketer telling consumers exactly what they need to be sexy, powerful, or successful.

This concept of visualization is one of the main reasons realtors encourage you to stage your home when you're trying to sell it. Once the buyer envisions himself or herself in the space, living there, sitting on the couch watching TV, or sitting at the dining room table eating breakfast, you are that much closer to a sale.

Think about how you approach making any major life decision in your own life: buying a car, purchasing a home, deciding whom you are going to marry. In all these cases, you spend time "trying it (or him or her) out." You test-drive the car, tour the home, and go out on dates. You want to make sure you can see yourself being content with your choice in the future and that it will fulfill your needs and your vision of how you want your life to be.

This applies to even small purchases such as clothing. The long-standing tradition has been to go through the exercise of taking an

145

article of clothing into the dressing room and trying it on for size—or to ensure that the store or website has a very liberal return policy.

The new world of marketing and product development is clearly very different. Instead of creating a vision that makes the consumer want to own your product, use your service, or participate in your experience, it's now the *brands'* turn to "try on" the consumer's core drivers and motivation and to see their product, service, or brand from the *consumer's* perspective, or rather how it benefits consumers and fulfills their unique needs.

This might sound like a daunting task. However, doing the work to ladder your consumers and unlock their DNA means that you will know them in a deep and authentic way—and more important, as more than just a demographic or segmentation. You will have the same information about your consumers as you know about your closest relatives or friends, people for whom you can always pick out the right gift or predict their reaction to a piece of news. It will be less like the relationship you have with, say, your second cousin who invited you to her wedding, clearly a case where it's more difficult to buy an appropriate and meaningful gift.

The new consumer seeks brands, products, and experiences that *already* feel like them. They have no interest in brands that attempt to convince them through manipulation or idealism that their product is the right one for them.

You can and should use the knowledge you've uncovered during laddering to start building your products and marketing messages from the consumer's perspective. In fact, this is the most important and most rewarding result from taking on such a project. It's the pot of gold at the end of the rainbow.

Unfortunately, I've found that this is also the step that most companies overlook and underutilize. They view the process of understanding their consumer groups merely as something to check off in their project plan. I can't say that I completely blame them, because most are still depending on unreliable and old-school research techniques such as focus groups or surveys. As a result, they 1) don't build methods for purposefully and systematically including the knowledge gained in their overall process and 2) the methods they are using provide unreliable results that can easily be misinterpreted or misunderstood.

To conduct laddering work on your consumers and never use it is like building a beautiful house and choosing to never live in it. What's the point of doing all that work if you aren't going to enjoy or benefit from it somehow?

You should benefit from it, of course, and this chapter will show you how. The exercises within will help you view and understand the world through your consumers' eyes by using a process I call lensing (see Figure 7.1).

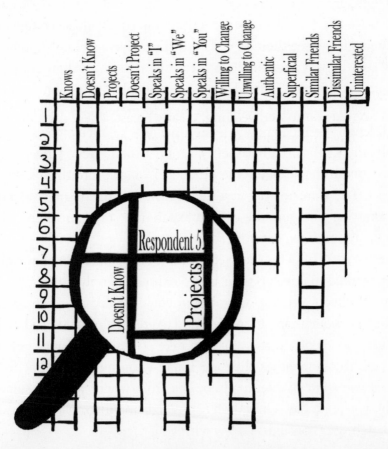

Figure 7.1   Use Lensing to Apply Consumer DNA to Your Initiatives

Understanding Your Brand

For lensing exercises to work effectively, you must truly understand who your brand is to your consumers and where you stand in relation to them. This might require some tough love.

Companies build words, messages, visuals, and mood boards to relate their overall objective for how they want the public to view both the company and the individual brands underneath its larger umbrella. This information guides the type of advertising they produce, the products they build, and even the feel of their stores or product displays.

Some companies that do this well include Apple, Target, Gap, and the Coca-Cola Company, to name a few. You already know that a message or advertisement is coming from one of these companies before you ever see their logo. These brands have a close alignment between the way that they see themselves and how their consumers see their brands. Take Target, for example. It has done a great job of taking discount to a whole new level and uses its branding to differentiate its company from other like retailers, for example, Walmart, K-Mart, Dollar General, and Dollar Tree. Target even takes time to repackage some products to make sure they feel like Target. The company has invested a great deal in consumer experience testing to ensure the overall experience stays consistent with what consumers expect from them.

However, Target is the exception, not the rule. Most companies have worked to develop their brand expression only internally. As such, it reflects a highly aspirational view but doesn't often reflect reality. Although aspirations can lead to great things—indeed, both Target and Apple initially had to take an ambitious approach to become the companies they are today—you must start not from where you want to eventually be but from where your consumers think you are today. Only then can you define the steps it will take to match your consumers' view with your view.

To determine what this is, ask yourself and your team: What words would our consumer really use to describe our brand? How would our brand appear as a person?

For example, you might need to distinguish what your brand aspires to be (for example, hip and cool) from what it is today (stodgy and staid). That doesn't mean you can't get to where you want to be, but you have to start with who and what you currently are.

It's a lot like the process of trying to lose weight or get into better shape, and it's something you know won't happen overnight. You have to assess where you are today by determining what you are doing right and what you are doing wrong and then develop a plan that will get you to your ideal state sometime in the future with a plan and milestones to get there. No miracle drug, patch, or contraption is going to circumvent the hard work required—just as no specific marketing campaign will change the public's perception of your brand overnight. You need to think about the current state of your relationship with the consumer in the same way. Understand and accept your consumers' perception; then determine what it takes to move closer to them, not to try to make them move closer to you.

When you walk into a cocktail party or any other social event, you are naturally drawn to others you already know or have an affinity toward. Consumers interact with brands and products like they do with other people at a cocktail party. They tend to spend the most time with their closest friends—the ones they already have an affinity toward. We form snap judgments about those we are meeting for the first time, and we do the same with new brands. Consumers carry with them a set of well-ingrained opinions about the brands that have been around for a while, and it takes work to change their perception.

The way your customers perceive your brand and product attributes is a far more important aspect in their decision making than your offering's features, functions, or even quality. These aspects are a given and easy to compare for the consumer. They will weed out an inferior product well before it makes it into their ecosystem. I recently heard a marketer at a conference make a seemingly obvious yet still significant statement: "Being good or reliable is a given. No one buys your car or product because it starts. That is expected." Therefore, you must deliver something far more compelling and meaningful to consumers to make it worth their time and attention.

Breaking Down Internal Barriers

Consumers see your company and your brand as one cohesive entity, so what one part of the organization does has an impact on their overall perception. This is why you must direct the development of a relationship with the user, and the process of really understanding who that person is, from the top of the organization down.

If you only fix a specific problem with a message, a product, or a customer service issue but fail to affect change across the organization, you haven't really corrected the problem at all. It doesn't matter how great a product or service is if the teams selling and supporting it don't view the consumer holistically and from the consumer's perspective.

My experience tells me that companies work too much in silos. And although each silo is responsible for fixing their part of the equation, they rarely pass information they learn over to other groups. For instance, marketing may learn that consumers don't understand a certain word or phrase being used in the company documentation, but they never pass this information along to their customer service group or sales representatives. Even if they do share, it tends to be watered down from what they'd originally learned.

I often see companies viewing themselves as specific internal silos as well. Consumers don't understand the makeup of your organization, and honestly, they don't care. They want your company, from the time they first interact with you until they complete a transaction, to understand them holistically.

Companies don't do this out of spite, of course. Teams frequently have to do more with less, so they do their very best to meet the objectives they've been given within the areas they can control. To create a real impact, you have to put a system in place, the same way you would with manufacturing or technology departments that fosters and shares new information from user interactions across the company's ecosystem. The system needs to be driven from the top down and consumer information needs to be available centrally to all of the systems that run the company. Disney and Zappos are two well-known examples of companies that are consumer-focused from their executive team down. This focus and attitude is built into their company's culture.

Influence and Affirmation Has Changed the Buyer's Journey

In the new economy, consumers choose entirely on their own to include a product or service in their inner circle; they will then will look to influencers to help affirm this choice. This is a common modern-day use of social networks both online and in person.

For example:

- *Pre–Mass Customization:* Vicky sees her friend Cathy using a product or wearing a new brand and asks Cathy where she got the product. If you watch a movie from the 1980s, you can see this obsession with and focus on status brands such as Chanel, Gucci, or Member's Only jackets throughout. Vicky then goes to the store to buy the same thing. She has been influenced by Cathy's purchasing decision, and Vicky is making her choices based on a desire to fit in with Cathy.
- *Post–Mass Customization:* Vicky hears about something new regarding a brand or product. This messaging might appear on

her favorite blog, in her Twitter feed, on a Pinterest board she follows, or in an article by someone that she knows and trusts has written. She decides that it feels like her and she then looks to Cathy for a final affirmation before making the purchase. Vicky is making her own choices here; she's merely checking with others to affirm her choice and vouch for the brand or product.

Vicky's decision is driven by the messages that make their way into her ecosystem. This is precisely why delivering the *right message* at the *right time* across the *right channel* within an established relationship is crucial for influencing Vicky. And these messages are unlikely to be traditional marketing messages. This may take the form of a story she reads that discusses how the brand helped someone else out, an interaction she sees between the brand and a friend of hers in which the brand is being helpful, or, really, any representation of the brand or product that gives Vicky a reason to be interested or relate.

This alignment in the post–mass customization era is displacing the traditional sales representative and has forever changed the buyer's journey. One of the most interesting parts is how it is turning everything we're used to on its head. More complex products that used to require a higher-touch sales approach now need transactional sales, whereas transactional sales items need relationships.

For example, think about how we buy cars now versus the way we used to only few short years ago. Buying a car used to be quite an ordeal. The consumer would visit multiple dealerships, spend time driving different cars, try to muddle through the available information in brochures and car manufacturer–created content, and listen to the salesperson's pitch to determine which car would really fit his or her needs.

All the research, knowledge, and insight we need to buy a car now is at our fingertips thanks to blogs, websites, and content available on social media sites. The sales rep has become a mere order taker.

For example, I own an RV and needed to buy a replacement vehicle to pull it. I was in negotiations for a Mercedes Benz GL450. All the specs for the vehicle indicated it could pull the RV without a problem and do an even better job than the vehicle it was replacing. The sales rep with whom I was working assured me that it could accomplish this task without a problem, but I wanted to verify this for myself. One of the biggest barriers I had to overcome was that I couldn't find a single picture of a GL450 pulling an RV anywhere on the Internet. I finally decided to buy the GL450 and immediately posted a picture of it pulling my RV (which it does incredibly well) so that others would feel comfortable making the same decision.

Selling Power magazine publisher Gerhard Gschwandtner recently predicted that the number of salespeople in the United States could decline from the current 18 million to around 4 million by 2020. He quoted a Gartner report that projected that 85 percent of the interactions between businesses will be automated by that time, without any need for human interaction. This statistic certainly has the potential to be true. Think about it: the purchaser has everything needed to make a decision before stepping into a store or talking to a salesperson. The salesperson becomes a final checkmark, not the *reason* the consumer makes the decision. In other words, the big risk for a salesperson is the potential to deter a sale, not encourage it.

Understanding what consumers want to hear and don't want to hear from your brand or company is crucial to maintaining or changing who they perceive your company to be.

Stop Trying to Change Consumer Behavior

Much to my dismay, I often hear and see companies attempt to prevent their consumers from shopping multiple sites before making a decision. This is a waste of effort. We have at our deepest core a desire to hunt, compare, and rationalize. No matter the promises or the guarantees included throughout a site, it is human nature to look at multiple sources before deciding whether something is true or correct. Only the truly loyal are already going to buy from your site with very little comparison. It's just as hard to make a loyal consumer shop somewhere new as it is to prevent a non-loyal consumer from performing comparisons.

Let's say that your consumer is collecting points or has some level of prestige with your organization. That particular individual won't spend very much time comparing you with other brands and sites. Because I am an Atlanta resident, where Delta Airlines is headquartered and is an important part of our city's heritage as well as the most prevalent airline, I am loyal to Delta. As long as its nonstop price from Atlanta to the location I am headed is within $50 of the other carriers, I am going to book with Delta. I will do a comparison using one aggregator and will immediately gravitate toward a Delta choice. Money is something that consumers always cite as a factor in their decisions. However, as I discussed earlier in this book, it's more important to understand the consumer's view and relationship to money than to focus on the actual cost. You must remove cost as a deciding factor during laddering and lensing exercises and apply it as a filter only *after* you're done understanding the core drivers.

Consumers quickly sort and organize companies, brands, products, and services into mental buckets—and then keep them there. It is extremely difficult to alter someone's perception of what you are good at or known for. Although some big names such as Apple have achieved this by becoming a music, book, and video store, this is not a feat many companies can accomplish—and Apple didn't do it overnight. It's far better for you to become the very best at whatever the consumer views you as than to risk trying to become something your consumer believes you are not.

When you recognize the ways your consumer chooses to interact with your brand or company, embrace it; don't fight it. Instead, learn how to capitalize on these preferences. Many brands make the mistake of ignoring a channel (e.g., Twitter or Facebook), and once you ignore it for too long, it is difficult—in fact, usually impossible—to recapture.

Staying Top of Mind versus Acquisition and Support

Some brands are using digital experiences and sponsorship to keep their product top of mind for users. If this is your marketing's primary aim, lensing exercises help you evaluate where to place this content, as well as what it should (and shouldn't) contain to appeal to the right clusters. For instance, if your product is funny or quirky, the top-of-mind experiences need to be aligned with that. Trader Joe's and Old Spice are both examples of brands that do a great job of embracing and promoting their brand message. Grocery store chain Trader Joe's has always known who they are, from the quirky newsletter they send out to their handwritten price signs throughout the store. Similarly, male grooming products maker Old Spice is a good example of one that went from "your father's brand" to one that has been embraced by a younger set. This occurred largely thanks to a unique and well-orchestrated marketing campaign featuring the Old Spice Guy and, more recently, Italian fashion model Fabio. Old Spice accomplished this top-of-mind currency by accepting who they were and moving themselves across the consumer chasm to enter the ecosystem of a new group of consumers.

If your brand is caring or high touch, reaching out on birthdays and other important events makes sense. A brand that is utilitarian, like your power company or cell phone provider, not so much.

The new rules of acquisition and staying top of mind will mean different things to different clusters. Some want information concisely and quickly, whereas others trust third parties over receiving information directly from the company even if the information is exactly the same.

Content Source and Distribution Are Paramount

I have determined during lensing exercises that companies often need to create and distribute the same content through two different channels: one channel branded as from the company and the other, from a third party. Although the content is exactly the same, the *source* is so highly crucial to the various clusters' sense of trust and relationship that it must be delivered different ways.

The same is true with support—that is, different clusters need different levels of support, but not in the way that is traditionally established. You'll recall from the BellSouth case study cited after Chapter 2 that there were clusters of individuals who wanted to be taught how to solve the problem as part of the support process. Other clusters cared only about having the problem fixed as quickly as possible; they had no desire or requirement to understand why a problem occurred. When companies establish support teams, they often default to first-, second-, and third-level support based on the severity of the problem. They fail to consider the much more crucial elements: the consumer's perceptions and core DNA.

Lensing will help you figure out exactly who needs and wants what by mapping certain types of users to certain support channels and content. By using lensing, you can craft the right messages to reach out to your user communities and determine the priority you are placing on different support channels. A decision to ignore a channel may be a decision—albeit an uninformed one—to cut off one of your clusters. And once you become known for ignoring or abusing a channel, it's almost impossible to repair the damage that's been done.

One company I work with is constantly responding to their user clusters using the word *free*. But because this is a higher-priced brand, consumers who buy from it don't care whether something is free. The word *easy* would be more effective in this case. In addition, they often respond to consumers by lurking on different social media channels and replying to those complaining about their service, *without being invited to do so.* This will alienate certain consumer clusters from that channel and cause them to see the brand as out of touch, pushy, and clueless about establishing relationship. If this brand analyzed the follow-up messages between the consumers they are following through lurking, they would see how uncomfortable this makes certain people. By reading their profiles and the other information they share in their feeds, they could easily identify each consumer's cluster and understand the why behind that person's decisions.

Identify the Primary and Secondary Clusters

It is critical to identify the primary cluster for any given product or campaign—and no, it cannot be everyone. Which cluster is either closest to the product or most likely to resonate with the campaign? This becomes your primary group for your lensing exercise. It's fine to choose a secondary cluster, as it can be necessary and appropriate for reach. Make sure, however, to keep this secondary group in the proper place when performing your evaluation.

Two ways of using the results of laddering and latticing is through standard lensing exercises such as brainstorming and evaluation.

Brainstorming

Lensing exercises support powerful brainstorming sessions with your team. You can use the information you have learned about your consumers to prioritize information from the user's perspective. Start by blue-skying the concept you are considering working on, just as I outlined in Chapter 5. But this time, perform the blue-sky activity from the perspective of the cluster.

If you are selecting primary and secondary clusters, you can assign half of your team to play the role of the primary cluster and the other half to play the secondary cluster. This creates a natural and important conflict in the process that requires the team to think about the new idea from the consumers' perspective, not their own. Proceed in the same manner as you did for confirming clusters, but use the *consumer DNA* you've gained to vet the ideas and determine why an idea might or might not work. You should conduct end-of-process voting from the perspective of the cluster, not the participants' point of view.

It's best to hold this type of brainstorming session using cross-functional teams, composed of members who touch the consumer at different points throughout their life cycle, from awareness to support. Part of what the marketing department and product development teams of the future must do is break down the barriers between the different internal groups. Consumers buying from you don't see these kinds of internal divisions, nor do they care about them. You are one brand and one company in their mind, so that's what you must strive to be in reality as well.

It was in one such brainstorming exercise that a participant suggested gun ranges as a stress relief option (see Chapter 5). I stated before that this seemed like an outrageous suggestion, but we put it on the board anyway. And good thing we did because when we evaluated it from the primary cluster's needs and core drivers, it created a flow that produced a whole set of potential services, including spa and beauty services and golf outings. Although that specific recommendation didn't make it into the final cut, without it, we might have missed an entire section of ideas that led to a successful solution that met the cluster's core need which was access.

Once you are done with the brainstorming session, sort the ideas into buckets of like items. Then use a voting system from the perspective of the cluster to reduce the number of items down to about 10 percent of the original suggestions. You can use this narrowed list to test concepts with your clusters and understand what's truly important to them.

I know that I discouraged focus groups earlier. However, this is a good time to reintroduce them into the mix. Just remember to recruit your participants based on the clusters—not their segmentation or demographic characteristics—and let the participants lead as much of the ideation session as you can, rather than trying to guide them yourself. Remember, the consumer is the expert. You should use these precious opportunities to extract as much as you can from them to learn how to truly establish and maintain a relationship, and drive your product and service ideation.

Evaluation

Once you understand what your consumers really want, you can begin to evaluate every campaign through their eyes. You will empathize with how they will experience the campaign, what words you need to use, how they will react, and what stumbling blocks they may face. For instance, I do not know how to be a 40-year-old female with two kids and a mini-van. However, thanks to the work I have done laddering consumers, I do know how to be someone who likes authentic experiences; is interested in projecting herself but guarded by what she says; prefers to speak in first person; likes to spend money but think she is saving; and shares online, because she is more connected and comfortable there than in person.

I use many techniques for lensing based on the maturity of the idea or concept. I've found that more concrete the concept or idea is, the more concrete the evaluation can and *should* be. Some techniques that work well for performing lensing evaluations include:

- *SWOT:* A simple strengths, weaknesses, opportunities, and threats analysis goes a long way to identify what parts of a concept or idea are solid and determine what you might need to do to either make the concept work or decide it's a bad idea altogether. Simply review your primary consumer cluster's key tenets or drivers, and start to list the attributes in these four different categories. If you find it difficult to sort the aspects or elements of what you are evaluating in this way, simply draw a line down the middle of the page and create a pros and cons list.

Example: Let's say you are evaluating a new television show that is going to run during prime time. You can use a SWOT analysis to determine not only the primary and secondary consumers (clusters) who will be naturally drawn to the show but also where to promote the show and how to interact with the audience while it airs. If the show has a behind the scenes element, Passionate Penny will love it. Chatty Cathy won't care because it won't help promote her own personal brand. Vice Vicky will be drawn to an edgier show that exposes the underbelly of society, while Cautious Callie wants something safer and more feel good in nature.

- *News Reporter:* This is especially helpful when thinking through a brand-new concept and determining what's necessary to meet the targeted consumer cluster's needs. Answer all the same questions about the idea that a reporter would have to. Determine the *who, what, when, where, why,* and *how* of the idea. Then look for gaps or incongruities in the story, specifically in terms of what drives the consumer cluster to an awareness, participation, or acceptance of something new.

Example: Let's say that you have created a brand-new product that will fundamentally change the way people perform a certain task. The first group you would go after to help you spread the word is Cool Cade. He needs to experience it firsthand, so you need to answer all the questions about how you draw Cool Cade into an authentic experience with this new product. Once Cool Cade has had time to play with the technology in an authentic way, build a way for it to be released to your less involved but more vocal groups.

We worked with one client who was undergoing the process of creating a campaign for a brand. The plan was to create a scavenger hunt to promote the product. However, we faced a problem: the product primarily appealed to a consumer cluster whose core DNA included a desire for things to be easy. These consumers had to be affirmed by others in their ecosystem, and they preferred safe, predictable experiences. Therefore, a fundamental change was required to get them to participate in this campaign. One possibility was to release the campaign to a smaller but more likely to participate group. However, the marketing department had to accept the fact that they would have to wait for results. They ultimately decided to approach this consumer cluster with an easy-to-share (and affirm) question about their favorite topic: themselves.

- *Artifact Idol:* This works well to narrow an idea's concepts when you're considering its impact on multiple clusters. Ask different members of your team to judge the concept from the cluster's unique perspective. That way you can understand how to introduce the idea and what it might take to get it to move across the different groups successfully.

  Example: You are creating a marketing message that is meant to be far-reaching and appeal to multiple clusters. Allow team members to assume the role of each cluster you are targeting and provide feedback about what they like, don't like, understand, and don't understand from their cluster's perspective. By looking for positive overlaps and recognizing the incongruities, you can predict the success and determine where you might need to fill gaps.

Depending on the situation, there are many other activities you can perform that are similar to the ones described here. Look to standard focus group or brainstorming activities as a starting point, and think through how it might be modified for a lensing approach.

Again, it's best to perform all these activities using cross-functional teams. Each person and group brings unique subject matter expertise and thoughts to the activity. When describing the attributes of the consumer clusters, I often see members of the sales team say things like, "Oh yeah, I've met that guy before," or support staff employees state, "That sounds like the last person I helped on the phone." As a result, these exercises make the consumers *real* to your employees, something that goes a long way in getting them to start thinking about their work differently.

The Result—Actionable Project Briefs, Product Roadmaps, and RFPs

Writing a project brief or plan to move forward after a lensing exercise makes the components truly actionable for members of a design, creative, development, or implementation team. Instead of receiving a generalized set of instructions for what to build, they have a specific direction in which to go with information on the elements they need to include in the process—and why. The brief serves as a highly valuable roadmap to which the team can refer back during the development process and continue to reference to make sure they are on track.

The results of lensing create a solid set of requirements that can be used to inform any new technology selection, process implementation, or improvement. You can craft incredibly powerful requests for proposal (RFPs) with this information at your team's fingertips. The ultimate vendor selection should be based on a solution that will best fit the intended consumers' needs.

Lensing is one of the most powerful and important outcomes of laddering your consumers. Indeed, it's the goal: to be able to deeply understand your consumers and evaluate everything you plan to do from their point of view is what will separate your organization from the rest. It allows your team to work hand in hand with consumers and build exactly what they want and need. It's a fundamental change in the way your organization approaches its work—an outward-in look at all the initiatives, campaigns, and product launches you undertake. Most important, to survive and thrive in today's mass customization world, it's the step all companies must take or risk being left to languish in old, dying paradigms.

In the next chapter, I will discuss how to socialize your laddering and lensing work throughout the organization to support a fundamental change in thinking.

Key Points

- Lensing is one of the most powerful aspects of laddering, because it puts your team in your consumers' shoes.
- You must be honest about where you stand with your consumers to properly bridge the gap from where you are to where you want to be.
- For the lensing process to work properly, you may need to break down some internal barriers that prevent knowledge from being shared across the entire organization.
- The buyer's journey has been fundamentally and permanently altered. As a result, consumers make their own decisions and look for affirmation after a purchase or decision.
- The rise of choice, avenues for product use and selection, make it impossible to change consumer *behavior*. Companies must instead learn how to exist within their consumers' behavior patterns and build products and services that meet consumers' individual needs.
- The approach for acquisition, staying top of mind, and providing support is very different than it used to be. You must deploy different lensing approaches and establish different measurements of success.
- You must lens with a primary cluster in the forefront while being mindful of how the secondary cluster is affected and what their level of participation is.
- Lensing will result in actionable and measurable initiatives for your team to help the company move forward.

8

Practical Application of Laddering

Knowledge without application is like a book that is never read.
—Christopher Crawford, Hemel Hempstead

I HAVE ALWAYS been curious about collectors—people who go around buying things that will never be used. I will be honest; I don't entirely understand them, or why they engage in this hobby. I've always wondered things like, "What good is a Barbie doll that stays in its box and never fulfills its greater purpose of having a young girl dress it up and play with it?" and "Why bother owning a set of china (or multiple sets, for that matter) that stays on a shelf and is never used to serve a meal?"

I feel the same way about the knowledge we gain about our consumers when we do rich-quality work to understand who they are and then never bother to use it or update it, instead choosing to generally ignore it. Many organizations that commission consumer discovery projects still work in an older model where they merely talk to consumers for the sole purpose of being able to claim that they've conducted consumer research. Or, they authorize a deep understanding of their consumers only to do nothing in terms of acting upon the results. They fail to realize that information like this can be your strongest asset in today's changed environment, just as important as the facilities you build, the employees you hire, and the technology you purchase.

Back in the days of VHS tapes and limited bandwidth, we used to deliver research to our customers in a physical box. Just like the Barbie doll, it was put on a shelf, never to be used again.

The recent rise of the individual has brought with it the complexity of new ways to market to consumers. Specifically, it added complexity to our ability to establish and maintain authentic relationships. The good news is that once you have completed the process of laddering, latticing, and lensing your consumers, you will have a strong understanding of how to move forward in many areas that have been a struggle for companies in recent years.

167

One of the most successful ways to make this work for your organization is to bring the knowledge you have gained to life, to take the information off of the shelf and actually use it. The following are some steps that can help you bring your consumers to life for your organization.

Bringing the Consumer DNA to Life

1. *Take stakeholders through a short version of the journey you took to ladder and understand your consumers.* Share some of the key questions you used to identify and sort each of the clusters. To help make this interactive, you can have a couple of unsorted consumers. Then have the people to whom you are presenting sort these consumers into appropriate clusters. This exercise helps make your sorting method understandable to others, uncovers any gaps in their knowledge or your explanation, and quickly corrects any misconceptions of what makes each cluster unique.

   This presents the opportunity for your team members to experience a compelling result: they may begin sorting themselves into clusters. Self-identification is a very powerful way to bring the clusters to life. Another interesting phenomenon that can happen is encountering a naysayer or challenger in the audience. When given the opportunity to talk with those types of people about their concerns, I usually find they don't like the cluster to which they most closely belong.

2. *Use real pictures and an easy name to represent the cluster.* To make this interactive and impactful, build posters for each cluster. Make them large enough that everyone in the room can clearly see them, and use real pictures of consumers you talked with, not stock pictures. This tool is a great way to represent your various consumers and have them right there with you as a constant reminder and reference point throughout the

presentation and lensing activities. It is also helpful to leave these behind in order to socialize the clusters throughout the company.

Give each cluster a catchy name, and make sure it includes two elements: a word that describes a primary driver for the cluster and an easy-to-remember personal name that starts with the same letter. You might recall Relaxer Ronald as one of the travel clusters from Chapter 6's case study. You immediately know that Ronald likes to relax, and that fact remains in the forefront of your mind as you think about him and think from his perspective.

3. *Create a simple narrative for each of the personas.* An engaging way to present the narratives is to have different people (that is, not just you) record a reading of each. Then you can play it for the audience, which helps make that cluster come alive for the group. A narrative for Chatty Cathy might sound something like this:

My TV has to be live, so that I can put in my two cents. I'm opinionated and love discussing my favorite shows. I don't like being left out of the conversation. I watch TV every evening and always have my phone, tablet, or laptop nearby because I love to text, tweet, or even chat while I am watching. I definitely keep up with who is watching what and the newest updates. I am on Facebook and Twitter all the time. I check in to locations, post updates, make comments, and tweet throughout the day. I love keeping up with Twitter during events like the Grammys; everyone is online, and my friends and I can comment on fashion, performances, and commercials. This is a great time to find new people to follow—and, of course, to pick up new followers of my own.

4. *Create e-mail addresses for the clusters.* One way to keep a cluster alive is by sending out notes using each cluster's perspective.

If an event takes place—for example, a roundup of the commercials that run during the Super Bowl—you can send out an e-mail reaction to the advertisements from each of the clusters. You can discuss what resonated with them, what didn't, and what each cluster's reaction to the campaign is. Use pop culture, current events, and media to reinforce your clusters to your team and to remind them that the clusters represent a living ecosystem that has a set of reactions and expectations to the world around them.

I have even seen companies build life-sized images of the clusters and place them around the office to help everyone remember who their consumers are. Alternatively, they kick off a product brief with the picture of the clusters at the top of the page and as either a letter to the cluster or a letter from the cluster's perspective. You want to use whatever unique techniques and methods you can come up with to keep these clusters top of mind and driving the organization's daily decisions.

Practical Applications of Laddering Knowledge

The next part of this chapter will cover some unique ways to approach your consumer groups, methods that support their growing desire for authenticity and move your company from one that is merely transactional to one that fosters understanding and relationship. The good news is that once you have done the work to understand your user groups, you will know what methods make the most sense, as well as which messages and modes to use for distribution.

You won't be guessing; you will have *proof* that supports the best approaches. Furthermore, you'll be aware of what you need to track on the back end to see if your actions are working. You will track more than the number of downloads or hits; you will also be able to know *when* that information is important (and when it's not).

Content Is King

Since the dawn of the Internet, online pioneers have been shouting "Content is king" from the rooftops. They've done it so much that marketers have become numb to the message.

However, I am here to tell you that in today's consumer-driven economy, content truly *is* king.

What you say, how you say it, the tone in which you say it, and where you say it make a huge difference to your message. And the amount of time you have to capture a consumer with a given message is so finite that you better be taking advantage of *every* opportunity. You aren't usually risking alienating your consumers; what you risk is being completely and deftly *ignored* with no understanding of why. Words matter. Images matter. Content matters.

As you have probably surmised based on the different types of *consumer DNA* I have shared, you can't use the same words (or images) for all of your user clusters. Recall the cruise line example discussed in Chapter 3. You would utilize the content about the brand to start funneling cruisers toward the elements they really care about. Specifically, you would do so by presenting equal amounts of content for all three drivers on the site's main page or in the cruise line's marketing materials: destinations, leisure, or the on-board party.

As each cluster self-selects into the content that matters most to them, you can begin to understand what they really care about. This understanding allows you to provide enhanced content about their main driver. Make sure to give them some hooks back to other content in case they end up in an area accidentally or from a badly returned web search.

In Chapter 4, we focused on some different social TV clusters. Here, your application needs to quickly highlight what each cluster ultimately cares about. How does the application support Chatty Cathy's ability to find others to talk about the show and meet new friends?

What extra special information are you providing to Passionate Penny that she cannot get anywhere else? How are you getting her closer to the characters and actors she loves and wishes to understand more?

You may need to vary the tone of your words for different groups. Vice Vicky is fine with and actually prefers the use of negative language and crass humor. She doesn't have the time or the patience to tolerate complex or confusing language. You must therefore read her sentiment about a product or service through this lens. Although Vice Vicky may appear to be incredibly confident, she actually suffers from a high level of insecurity and wants nothing more than to fit in and prove her worth. Using her language and understanding what she really needs is the way to talk to her core DNA.

You may find within the *consumer DNA* that certain clusters want to:

- Hear about other people's previous experiences.
- Know what's happening now.
- See what's going to happen in the future.

Considering these three content approaches within your clusters or looking for patterns in what each one prefers while you perform laddering is the best way to ensure you've covered all of your bases.

Social Media Usage Is a Manifestation of Our Core

Social media has allowed us to do something that we haven't been able to do for the first time in over a century: connect with each other like we used to when society was built around small villages or communal groups. But today, instead of meeting around the local well or market to discuss the news of the day, we build our own network of like-minded people. We share what we find by knowing what is important to our network and based on what we know about one another. We don't rely on a larger organization to tell us what is important to us; we make that decision on our own. We've concluded that mass media has failed us too many times, and we seek confirmation from people that we trust. We listen to those with whom we've established relationships, people who we know are giving us important and true information.

Social media allows us to manifest who we are at our core. It's truly a forum where the way we speak and the information we post (pictures, blogs, comments, and so forth) is very similar to the way we would present ourselves in public.

Therefore, brands need to evaluate social media information from the user's perspective. We can't merely base our understanding on what's being said; we must understand who is saying it and what kind of impact that person really has on those in shared circles. Just because a brand is mentioned negatively doesn't mean it's a bad thing—if the cluster it attracts is a negative cluster. It is far more important to understand *who* made the comment and what prompted that person to do so. Is it within that individual's profile to use negative words or maybe no words at all? If you work for an edgy brand, using the filter of negative sentiment about what people are saying may not be the right way to view the context of a social media message. Understand that self-promoting clusters like Chatty Cathy may skew the interest in your content, message, or product because this group is entirely focused on self-promotion.

Importance of Engagement

The way forward is in the area of engagement. You want to provide valuable content and interesting information to tell your story to your consumer groups in a way that allows them to see your brand, service, company, or experience; instinctively understand it's identity; and see how it fits into their world.

This doesn't mean asking your consumers to like your page or retweet your post. It also means you must go beyond simply sending out e-mail blasts with information about your latest and greatest sale. When you spend time with friends, your goal is to come away a little better, a little more informed. What can your brand, company, or service to do in the same way to surprise, delight, educate, or inform your loyal consumers?

Laddering shows you how and when to speak to each of your consumer clusters, making the mystery of engagement less mysterious. It's the same as it is with any other friendship or relationship; once you've laid the groundwork, you naturally know what to do. And although this isn't difficult, it does require that you take a step back to define your own reasons why. *Why* are we sending out this message? What is the *purpose* of the campaign? What does it *do* for our consumer groups? If you find that the results of asking that question are all self-serving, that they merely push your agenda or ask the consumer to do something for you, then you need step back and rethink your strategy. One bad campaign or message can create an unexpected backlash.

Take fast food chain McDonald's, for example, which launched a social media campaign in January 2012 with the hashtag #McDStories. They were looking for responses that spread the good news of McDonald's, specifically to promote the creation of new jobs at their restaurant locations. But the hashtag was promptly hijacked by unhappy diners, who used it to tell horror stories about eating at the restaurant and getting sick and to perpetuate rumors about how McDonald's food was sourced and produced. It became a public relations nightmare for McDonald's and put the company on the defensive on many fronts.

McDonald's made two mistakes in this campaign:

1. *It was self-serving.* Telling a McDStory benefits only the company, not the consumer. A much better approach would have been to retweet stories, promote existing tweets they found in consumers' updates, or highlight a blog post about a good experience

at the restaurant. McDonald's could have taken advantage of what already existed to promote their brand instead of asking consumers to *like* them. Yes, it would have taken time to spread through the ecosystem, but it would have been more authentic, organic, and easier to manage than a promoted hashtag.

2. *No consideration was given to the different consumer clusters that might participate in such a campaign.* Just by the nature of its business, McDonald's attracts a wide range of consumer clusters, including a few that are not the most positive or reserved groups. Once the hashtag was hijacked for negative reasons, the conversation was less about McDonald's and more about who could post the most outrageous comment.

Beware the Sequel

One approach that simply no longer works is the formulaic approach to the world of marketing. That is, just because a campaign or method worked with one cluster of consumers or one brand doesn't automatically mean it will work again with the same group. I see marketers make this mistake often; they're looking for the easy solution and hit the rinse and repeat button. You need to understand why that blogger picked up your story or helped you spread your message the first time before you decide that person is your go-to guy or gal for the next iteration. You must analyze the scenario from every angle of your next endeavor's potential results and proceed accordingly.

Ask yourself, Did the blogger tell the story because it was original? If that's the case, then simply adding onto the story no longer hits the blogger's core driver. Did the blogger help you spread a message because there was some type of self-promotion in it for him or her? Did you provide exclusive content that made the blogger feel special and informed?

If you have done the proper work to understand your consumers, then undertaking a lensing exercise will help you vet the idea quickly and determine how to make it work. You will enjoy the payoff of the work you did unlocking your consumer's behavior into defined clusters.

There have been countless instances where I've met with clients in cross-functional teams, and because we already have a good understanding of their consumer clusters, we have been able to use a lensing exercise to kill an idea in a matter of 15 minutes. Many of these were concepts that would have traditionally gone forward. They sounded good on the surface and probably worked before for a similar brand. However, we knew that they wouldn't hold up once we viewed them from the intended consumer's perspective. And undergoing a lensing exercise to determine this early on is a *far* cheaper proposition than launching a campaign that ultimately fails.

Always remain focused on the why. Why did the campaign work? Why didn't it resonate with and among the consumer clusters? What you did and what happened as a result is great, but the why behind it is *golden*.

Word-of-Mouth Marketing

We may not remember the last advertisement we heard; however, we will talk about a story around a product or company for decades. As we move into a world of mass customization that is based on authentic relationships, storytelling is becoming a more important aspect to reaching the hearts and minds of consumers. These stories need to show up in consumers' daily lives and are the best way to reach some of the consumer clusters who do not actively participate in technology-based conversations—people like Everyday Eddie and Showless Joe, for example.

Nordstrom is famous for the story of the woman who returned a set of tires without question, even though Nordstrom doesn't sell tires. This story is repeated and repeated, yet very few people can tell you the contents of the last Nordstrom print ad or TV commercial they saw.

Word-of-mouth marketing involves storytelling. It requires that we look beyond what the product does to how it affects and improves the end consumer's life. The story has to be authentic and meaningful to those who are going to participate. It can't be an advertisement you force on consumers. Rather, it should be something you would tell at a dinner table or when you are out at brunch with friends, a story that would make those attending feel like they learned something new and interesting, not as though that they just had breakfast with a salesperson for the company.

Once you've established your *lattice construct* and know which ecosystems your clusters live in, you'll be able to identify how the stories will spread. Lensing provides the clues and components of a good story that is worth sharing. A story that doesn't seem like marketing and *isn't* self-serving.

The problem with word-of-mouth marketing and a relationship-based society in general is that they require marketers to have patience. It is not the same as launching a campaign, changing a price, adjusting a tagline, or creating a new version that focuses on value. In the past, these approaches might immediately create an uptick in the number of units sold or consumers participating in an experience. Relationships are developed over time, not in an instant. For something to be interesting and authentic, it can't be forced. A company needs to be willing to allow the time for the program to work over many months. This is especially true if the campaign's goal is to alter the public's perception of a brand or product from one they've held in the past.

By using the techniques I have outlined in this book, you'll be able to truly understand your consumers. You will be able to naturally identify and vet the stories that will resonate with your targeted clusters. You'll also gain insight into measuring early success with this type of approach, because you can listen to which clusters pick up the story and naturally share it for you. It even allows you the added breathing room of adjusting the approach or the story if it isn't hitting your consumer groups exactly right.

Unlocking Big Data for Smarter Conversations and Better Products

One final point: it doesn't matter how much big data companies collect on their customers. Collecting numbers is a desperate attempt to return to times gone by—a time when the mere collection of data and comparison of data to data led to a revelation that magically presented itself. This simply doesn't happen without a deeper understanding of the consumer. It's very likely that a company will take action on a false-positive or miss out on additional opportunity by making assumptions based only on data it's collecting.

Companies that fail to use a lens or key of consumer behavior to go *beyond* what big data alone indicate as a pattern will continue to build products and messages that miss the mark. Big data tells you only *what*; it's not until you know *why* that you're in the much stronger position of knowing what truly matters and what to do about it. Your consumer understanding needs to extend beyond preferences in color, previous buying behaviors, and brand affinity for the sake of brand.

As an example, many of our studies uncover consumer clusters that prefer to receive company-branded content, because they trust the company to provide the information. On the other hand, there will be clusters that prefer to resolve an issue or learn about new things by finding content provided from third parties. For some clusters, a third party could be an expert, *Consumer Reports*, or a movie critic, for example. For others, it's another like-minded person—not a company representative or a so-called expert, but someone who they relate to and trust.

When we run tests with the same exact content but brand one to the company and have a third party provide the other, the content tests more or less favorably depending on the group that we're querying.

This means that marketing needs to distribute content in many different ways—whether it's via the organization's traditional channels and/or through third-party resources that have the opportunity to tell the story. The company needs to support the clusters' core desire and allow the consumers to share the information the way they wish.

This is equally important for providing support to your consumers. A consumer who doesn't trust the company entirely will spend time on third-party sites trying to resolve an issue before reaching out to a support channel. Meanwhile, a more trusting consumer may spend substantial time on company-sponsored properties trying to find the answer independently.

If the company providing support to the end consumer can identify these consumer patterns in its big data, then it immediately knows how to speak to the end consumer in a way that fits that person's core behavior or desire. But if a brand fails to consider this possibility, it runs the risk of making assumptions about the consumer and infuriating that person during the support process, despite the company's best attempts in trying to resolve the problem. The company may end up recommending content that a consumer cluster will immediately discount and ignore because of the source.

Foursquare is a location-based social networking application first introduced in 2009 that allows users to use a mobile website to check in to various places they visit. The brand's creators discussed some patterns they noticed early on in a recent *Inc.* magazine interview. When they viewed the initial big data that their system generated, they noticed that many of the users saw a use for the application not as they had originally intended (checking into locations and collecting badges) but rather as a great way to get reviews and recommendations for locations around them. So instead of fighting this cluster's natural behavior, the creators embraced and celebrated it. After all, people were using their product; did it matter that it wasn't in the way they had initially envisioned?

Foursquare is one of my favorite examples of an application that has embraced the fact that different consumers use the application for different reasons. In addition to their flexible approach to supporting consumers' preferences, they also know how to use a single application to message and provide functionality that hits *four* core consumer behaviors: the desire to (1) become the "mayor" of a given location, an honor you receive from having checked in to a location more than anyone else, (2) receive unexpected rewards or discounts, (3) find out what other people might be at places near you, and (4) discover new and interesting places around your current location.

Many companies are following a somewhat disingenuous trend by trying to become more to the consumer than they really are, and they're doing so in an effort to collect more big data on their consumer clusters. For instance, they attempt to become a destination spot for their consumers for shopping and for information or services that are outside of their primary business focus. But these initiatives' ultimate goal isn't to know their customers better; rather, it's to sell the information they gain to other companies or data aggregators. Trying to be more to consumers than they need or want you to be is a tricky balance to strike. More often than not, your customers will quickly recognize this inauthentic attempt and thwart your efforts. One example of this is Facebook's attempt at building stores into the platform. We found in our studies that very few consumer clusters would consider shopping at a Facebook store. In addition, the clusters that would shop there are not the ones most brands are attempting to target, nor do they have the influence to drive other clusters to this type of adoption.

Following laddering techniques will put your company in a stronger position moving forward in the big data conversation. By taking the time to truly understand your consumer clusters—their desires, needs, and the elements that comprise their core DNA—you can better predict how to support them as technology and the marketplace grow and shift.

In the next chapter, I will discuss some emerging trends and how they will affect the changing relationship with consumers.

Key Points

- For your laddering work to have the greatest impact on your organization, you need to bring the consumer clusters to life for your company. Tell stories about clusters you met while performing the research, give the cluster an easy-to-remember name, create visuals that can be placed prominently throughout your organization, and give the clusters a voice.
- Apply your understanding of your consumers to every part of your organization.
- Keep in mind that as consumers seek more authentic relationships and understanding, content is more important than ever.
- Social media provides an unfiltered peek into many of your consumer cluster's core. You can therefore identify your consumer's DNA based on what they say and how they present themselves in their profiles.
- You absolutely must engage your consumers within their ecosystem and in the way they expect from your brand or company. Make sure that your engagement is focused on what you can do for the consumer, not just an attempt at getting the consumer to do something for you.
- The approach for acquisition, staying top of mind, and providing support is very different. You must deploy different lensing approaches and establish various measurements of success.
- Just because a program or campaign worked before doesn't mean it will again. You need to understand *why* it worked in order to determine potential future success.
- The rise of authenticity brings with it an appreciation of storytelling. Use stories to connect with your consumers and let them share your message for you.
- Collecting big data on your consumers just for the sake of collecting big data is a mistake. Use an understanding of your consumers to decide what to collect and how to analyze it.

BISSELL Word-of-Mouth Marketing Case Study

For marketers of the future to be successful, they need to understand how to insert themselves into their consumers' conversations when and where they're happening. Companies must illustrate how their product, service, or offering fits into and enhances those consumers' existing behavior. We can see one instance of this working successfully by studying the techniques implemented in a recent project by Atlanta-based agency Fizz, which specializes in word-of-mouth marketing. Fizz's goal was to increase vacuum cleaner and floor care product manufacturer BISSELL's overall sales of its BISSELL Sweeper, for which the company had been known since its inception.

BISSELL had designed its sweeper so elegantly from the outset that very few things had changed about it over the years. But this elegance also meant there was nothing new about the Sweeper—no compelling story that kept it top of mind for the consumer when considering a new floor cleaning purchase. And along with this lack of a compelling story came the obvious results: flat sales.

BISSELL Sweepers have always been known for handling in between cleans—the times that bringing out the larger vacuum cleaner didn't make sense. But the market for these types of products was crowded, and there wasn't anything that differentiated the BISSELL product from other available options or any reason to buy one over the other. Chief executive officer (CEO) and company legacy heir, Mark Bissell, didn't want to be the one to kill off the first product BISSELL ever created. However, unless sales—which were either flat or slowly declining year over year—didn't change, he knew he may have no other choice.

BISSELL took a unique approach to this problem by putting its existing product into a start-up within BISSELL that they called BBV. Start-ups are often known for building something new or innovative, which was the ultimate charter for the group. However, this approach differed in that the Sweepers would provide a revenue stream to help prop up this new group as it formed.

Fizz's CEO, Ted Wright, met with BISSELL to introduce the concepts of word-of-mouth marketing. BISSELL took these new philosophies and Fizz's belief in word-of-mouth marketing to heart. The BBV team moved its ad spend for the BISSELL Sweeper from broadcast to conversation-based marketing, keeping in mind, of course, that the conversation needed to be relevant and interesting for this to work.

Fizz spent time understanding what *really* made the product interesting. Yes, it was a great product for in between cleaning—this is the quality that the consumer base would traditionally cite if asked how they used the product. But what really set the BISSELL product apart was its ability to pick up what became known within the team's conversation as PITA pieces—"pain in the ass" pieces. Examples of these included LEGOs, pine needles, and cat litter. Interestingly, each PITA had its own special problem and associated user group:

- *LEGO Pieces:* The conversation around these PITA pieces was so widely known there is even an homage to stepping on a LEGO in the middle of the night at the LEGOLAND in California.

(continued)

(*continued*)

- *Pine Needles:* The number one reason many people need to buy new vacuum cleaners in January is because they spend December picking up pine needles, which secrete tiny amounts of sap, literally gumming up the internal works.
- *Cat Litter:* Cat lovers wanted to use something other than the main vacuum cleaner to clean up litter before their cats tracked it all over their house. After all, who wants to use the same vacuum cleaner to clean their carpets as they do for picking up urine- and feces-caked cat litter?

Because selling a sweeper is not the most interesting conversation on the face of the planet, Fizz had to determine where each of these commonly tied together groups congregated and figure out how to interestingly introduce BISSELL Sweepers as something that these groups would want to discuss.

For the first group, Fizz located the LEGO KidsFest, a company that travels from city to city renting out civic centers and selling access to parents and their children to come play with LEGOs for the afternoon. These events regularly attract more than 30,000 people per event. One area at the LEGO KidsFest is the brick pile, where children can play in a pile of LEGO bricks—literally millions of bricks. Once LEGOs are poured out into the middle of the floor, pieces begin to spread out from the inner circle. This then requires a constant battle to pick up these sidelined LEGO pieces and drop them back into the middle.

A unique feature of the BISSELL Sweeper is that it doesn't break LEGO pieces (very important to LEGO accessories, as Darth Vader's light saber will not survive a trip through the family's regular-size vacuum cleaner). Picking up the LEGO piece will also not break the sweeper, which is another added bonus. In addition, the clear plastic top lets the user know exactly where the piece is.

All of these advantages made introducing the BISSELL Sweeper into the LEGO KidsFest a fantastic opportunity. Fizz believed that once the parents saw how well the sweepers performed on this commonly cursed PITA, they would talk about it with other parents and pick one up for themselves the next time they were at their local store.

The unexpected result of this initiative was that the children attending the LEGO KidsFest event actually *liked* the sweeper. They were willing to stand in line to use it, much to the chagrin of the parent who had just paid ~$20 for them play with LEGOs. The parents got into the action by taking pictures of their kids using the sweeper and sharing it across their social media channels. This natural use of the product allowed BISSELL representatives to chat casually with the parents about the sweeper's features, thereby soft-selling them on the advantages of owning the product themselves.

These conversations continued well beyond the LEGO KidsFest events. The pictures the parents shared resulted in longer comment threads as the parents discussed the amazing ability of the sweeper to address this common problem. Parents shared the conversation at dinner—mostly in exasperation over the fact that they went to an event and their child spent substantial time waiting to sweep instead of just playing with the LEGOs. However, these talks always ended with, "It's amazing; I never knew the BISSELL Sweeper cleaned up LEGOs so easily."

As an added measure, Fizz identified the city's influential bloggers in each city before the start of the LEGO KidsFest

(continued)

(*continued*)

event. Fizz either sent the BISSELL Sweeper to these individuals to play with or sent them home from the event with it. However, they had absolutely no defined rules about what they had to do or not do with the product when they got home. It was completely up to these people to choose to write about the Sweeper or not. Many of them did, and one even made a video reenacting the dreaded stepping on a LEGO in the middle of the night scenario that went viral. They blogged about the story because it was authentic, interesting, and helpful. Many even listed the BISSELL Sweeper as one of their 10 favorite things of that year.

Fizz didn't follow the traditional model of setting up a booth and attempting to sell to people as they walked by. Rather, they sent people to collect the LEGO bricks and engage in spontaneous conversations. It was not a transaction or a sale but rather the establishment of a relationship.

Fizz used a similar technique to tackle the next PITA category: pine needles. They initially considered a partnership with outside tree sales lots like Big John's. However, they scratched the idea because the customer would be in and out, and it's not likely that people really care about pine needles being on the ground at an outdoor tree sales location. They opted instead for what can be one of the most excruciatingly boring tasks of the holiday season for a parent: a visit to see Santa Claus.

Fizz chose a widely popular Santa location, one with more than 6,000 appointments a year. They decorated a 300-foot-square area right next to the line for Christmas—complete with some pesky pine needles for brand ambassadors to sweep up as the line slowly crept by. If a bored kid asked to participate in cleaning up, the brand ambassador gladly stepped aside while the kid took over and the parents snapped picture after picture of their nicely dressed son or daughter gliding a BISSELL Sweeper over the pine needles. Fizz started getting creative with the pine needles, creating images and words that the children could then sweep up. They were careful to never force themselves on an individual; instead, they worked to establish relationships with the consumer in line and let *them* take the initiative to use the product and ask questions about it. The amazing result was that many of the kids added the BISSELL Sweeper to their Christmas list. It might not have been the first item on their list, but it made the cut as something they wanted under their Christmas tree from Santa.

The final venue for featuring the magic of the BISSELL Sweeper was at cat shows. This time, the Fizz team deployed a team of cleaners to clean up under the cages in the show's staging area. They also set up a booth that allowed pet parents to have pictures made with their feline children.

It was a bit more difficult to determine the influential members of this environment. Just like their beloved pets, cat people are naturally inquisitive; however, they wanted to approach the conversation on their own terms. They weren't lining up to use the BISSELL Sweeper in the way that the kids did at LEGOLAND or in the Santa lines; however, once the team had established trust with a few of them, the rest fell in line to understand the benefits the Sweeper could bring to their everyday lives. Soon, the Sweeper started showing up in blog and social media shares across the Internet as these individuals discussed their most recent discovery to keep themselves and their beloved pets clean.

Fizz's unique one-to-one marketing approach combined with BISSELL's willingness to take a chance on it provides a

(continued)

(continued)

perfect example of how to best capitalize on consumers' existing behavior to become part of their conversations and ecosystems. The result: a product that had been down for two years and steady for two more enjoyed a staggering 48 percent growth in the following two-year period. BISSELL made no other modifications to the product. There was no need to improve the features or change the design. BISSELL didn't use gimmicky coupons or inflate its sales by changing the price point. It simply changed the way it interacted with its consumers—and that made all the difference.

9

The Way Forward

You must learn a new way to think before you can master a new way to be.

—Marianne Williamson

As I SAID at the beginning of this book, I love change. And that's good news for me and people like me because the changes in the landscape for marketing and product development are definitely not over. We are just at the beginning of a new awakening about how to successfully develop new products and flourish during the rise of relationship marketing. Using the same old approaches to consumer engagement and acquisition with ever-diminishing results won't be acceptable much longer.

One of this book's primary purposes is to alter marketing departments and product/brand managers' perspectives—to shift their focus from what *has* happened to what *will* happen with their consumers. Therefore, I want to use this chapter to cover some trends in the consumer space, all of which support the notion that we must continue to strive to understand, support, and speak to consumers at their core.

The Control of Consumer Preference

The National Do Not Call Registry was established in 2004 to prevent telemarketers from interrupting our peace and quiet while we were at home trying to have a meal with our families or simply relaxing. Although many people aren't aware, there are Internet and wireless device versions of the do not call list that strive to prevent marketers from the same annoying tactics and breaches to personal privacy that can occur within other technology-based media. Legislation has been proposed that, once passed, would prevent tracking that marketing departments are currently conducting on what people are doing. How consumers are being *opted in* to receive messages and communication from different products and brands is already regulated. As these regulations grow, marketers must enter into mutually desirable relationships with their consumers to continue to market to them.

191

It's difficult to track granular and identifiable information on most mobile devices because the same type of tracking elements available on websites are not available on all mobile devices or implementations. Considering that entire clusters of consumers predict that they may never own a traditional laptop or desktop computer, as well as the chance that what we currently carry as technology may fundamentally change yet again in the near future, marketers must consider their approach to collecting and acting on consumer data accordingly.

Under existing and proposed legislation, the consumer must understand and agree with the value they receive from providing their marketing communication preferences. They will control how and when brands track this information across their experiences. Marketers and product managers with this type of insight can use smarter methods for predicting consumer interests. Its becoming increasingly critical to get consumer permission to share and communicate with them.

There's a problem with the way that most companies manage customer preference today, and it lies in the way they choose to implement the consumers' ability to *opt in* or *opt out* of communication. Many companies use an approach that PossibleNOW, the leader in customer preference management, calls an atomic *opt out*. This means that they provide the consumer with a big switch that in essence unsubscribes the consumer from *all* company correspondence. Once turned off, it's challenging to get the consumer reengaged.

A far better approach, one that PossibleNOW has deployed as a preference center that includes options for all of a company's many diverse channels from e-mail to text message, is to capture the consumer at the point of choice and allow them to *opt down*—that is, to specifically select which correspondence to receive over which channels and at what frequency. This approach truly supports the ability to send a consumer the right message at the right time across the right channel.

Another problem that PossibleNOW's technology has resolved is that in order to make sure companies are both honoring consumers' preferences for communication and giving them something meaningful, companies must keep this consumer information centrally located and up to date. Centralization provides the diverse systems and business units that make up today's companies an easy way to access and act upon this information. PossibleNOW's technology makes tracking of consumer preferences worry free. Companies benefit from honoring their consumers' preferences and can use the preference information to better understand their consumers' desires.

In a world where few people even bother to answer their phones or pay attention to what they receive in the mail, e-mail and other electronic interactions are the primary channels by which companies can and should communicate with their consumers. My work has found that as long as there is an appropriate benefit for the exchange in the information provided, most consumers are fine with sharing both their behavior and preferences. Companies just need to be careful about how they handle the channels of communication that are currently open between them and their consumers. They don't want to risk shutting down their potentially most valuable and easy-to-capitalize-on mode of relationship.

Another benefit of consolidating preference data and customer behavior is that it is important to the analysis you use to unlock big data. Once you have collected consumers' preferences, you can influence the collection of preference data either by asking consumers directly (explicit preferences) or by drawing inference based on their behavior (implicit preferences).

There's yet another valuable bonus to figuring out what kind of communication your customers favor—one that goes beyond legal requirements and general goodwill. Doing so provides a company with yet another layer of information about customers' core desires, information that is critical to unlocking how to interact with them. Again, it's crucial to store this knowledge—just like preference data—in a central location. This allows all areas of the company to use the information with the clusters in the way those clusters prefer and appreciate.

Not Buying a Product; Buying My Product

One thing that consumers today want is the ability to customize a product down to the finest details, in essence to make *your* product *their* product.

Shark Tank, a show that's dedicated to shedding light into the mysterious world of raising money for new ventures, featured an ice cream business called eCreamery that was pitching its product on one particular episode. If you have ever wanted to create your own ice cream flavor, eCreamery may just be what you have been looking for. The brand's cofounders, Abby Jordan and Becky App, have been making custom-flavored ice cream and gelato since 2007. They brought their successful business into the Shark Tank in hopes of appealing to the sharks', and ultimately the viewing audience's, sweet tooth. The ladies even made a custom flavor with premium spicy dark chocolate for Mark Cuban that they named The Cubanero. Consumers can order their own custom ice cream from the store and have it sent via overnight mail to their house.

A more extreme example of consumers being able to buy their own customized products is what Audi is doing in the United Kingdom. Audi has built a car dealership unlike anything that exists anywhere else. They have no inventory; instead, car buyers use a computer to design the car they want. It appears on a screen in front of them at the actual size and dimensions the car will be when they receive it.

The large screens give the consumer the opportunity to walk around the car and get a feel for its size and other choices they are making. Once the consumer saves the car, it is then placed on order and delivered to the consumer's house when it's ready. The dealership has one of each type of car to let consumers test drive and get a feel for handling and other important aspects of that experience.

This is an example of consumer-based mass customization at its finest. The consumer gets exactly what's wanted and doesn't feel as if he or she is being talked into a car just because it happens to be on the lot. The dealership can focus on giving each consumer his or her ideal product without worrying about moving existing inventory. Audi is able to dramatically reduce the overhead costs that are usually tied up in land and inventory. The manufacturing plant builds the car exactly the way the consumer wants to buy it; a known buyer is waiting to take the product off the company's hands the minute it rolls off the assembly line.

This is a far cry from Henry Ford's "They can have any color, as long as it's black" approach. If a car company can embrace consumer-based mass customization, then it should be far simpler for other product, service, and marketing organizations to do the same thing.

Creating My Own Experience

The Coca-Cola Company has come a long way from producing only one product back in 1886 to where it is today. Not only does it sell a wide variety of products to support different tastes across the globe, but is has recently introduced the ultimate product for the creation of a consumer's own experience. The Coca-Cola Freestyle machine is a modern-day soda fountain that provides more than 100 beverage choices—all at the touch of a button. The innovative machine is rolling out across the world thanks to the Coca-Cola Company introducing it via its distribution partners. The product's major draw: it allows the consumer the ability to mass customize his or her drink while standing in the store.

The Coca-Cola Company shared some of the impacts this consumer-focused product has had for its restaurant partners on its website. According to Jennifer Mann, Coca-Cola Freestyle vice president and general manager, "We've proven pre-launch and in-market that when a restaurant [offers] Coca-Cola Freestyle, their traffic, incidence and beverage servings grow anywhere from single to double digits . . . additionally, the perceptions of the restaurant brand improves."

And it's not just the Coca-Cola Company making these claims; restaurant owners attest to it as well. Mike Walsh, who owns seven New York locations of popular chain Moe's Southwest Grill, has Coca-Cola Freestyle machines in his two newest locations. "Our customers love it," Walsh says. "Everybody was mesmerized by it when we opened our two new stores. It's definitely a good business driver."

The Moe's franchisee is now busy converting his other five stores into Coca-Cola Freestyle locations.

After testing Coca-Cola Freestyle in some of its stores in Florida, Georgia, and North Carolina, the Moe's chain saw comparable sales jump by 9 percent. As a result, Moe's now requires all new franchises to have Coca-Cola Freestyle inside.

What's interesting to me is the attention I know the Coca-Cola Company paid to the Freestyle machine's roll out. I remember the first time I saw one. My wife, daughter, and I came across it one day while having lunch at a Burger King near our home. We chatted back and forth about how cool it was, struggled with figuring out how to use it, and tasted a couple of combinations to see what we really thought of the flavor.

After we sat down, I noticed a man sitting at a table nearby writing very discreetly in a notebook. He was paying rapt attention to anyone and everyone who walked up to the machine, taking notes about their interactions. He was wearing a black jacket with a subtle Coca-Cola insignia on it. I don't know it for a fact, but as a fellow researcher, I suspect, Coca-Cola was doing what every company needs to and should be doing: watching its consumers interact with a new product idea or concept in the actual context it would be used. He didn't have to pay us; he didn't even have to ask any questions. He could simply observe our use and overhear our conversations. So many companies have the same opportunity to receive this unfiltered and valuable content. They just need to take the time to do so and have a process that allows them to take action later on within the walls of their company.

The Rise of Perfectly Imperfect

The great news for marketers and product managers is that consumers don't want or expect perfection—in much the same way we don't expect our friends to be perfect. And the more they see your brand, company, product, or service as a friend, the more they want to hear and understand the real deal. Creating a voice, sticking to what your consumers expect from your brand, and being okay with admitting that you aren't perfect is far more important than perfection.

Many of the most successful campaigns have capitalized on this imperfection. Charmin has been successful with a Tweets from the Seat campaign that highlights just that. It has played off of a concept that would typically be taboo by celebrating what its product does for its consumers.

This willingness to be authentic is refreshing and important to establishing a relationship. The campaign is indirectly related to Charmin's products; at no time do they use this handle to tell their customers to "buy more Charmin."

Desire for Connection and Authenticity

I can recall reading a book in the 1990s that warned of a future in which we didn't know our neighbors, an existence where we spoke to only a select few people and chose to isolate ourselves into tight-knit groups. Although this prediction has come true to some extent—many of us don't know our neighbors as well as people did in the 1960s and 1970s—the result hasn't been the kind of cocooning this book foresaw. I argue instead that it's been more of a broadening.

We now have the ability to connect to and be in relationship with people with similar tastes and interests who live all over the world. We can bond with virtual strangers based on all levels of tastes and interests and maintain bonds with people from all stages of our life. Rather than resulting in isolation, these disruptive technologies have allowed for a *stronger* connection among individuals.

Think about how various social network sites make this work. Pinterest supports the ability to follow others with the same tastes and interests. It allows us to connect with and share ideas for inspiration or aspiration. Facebook brings the widespread family back together by highlighting the events that are going on in others' lives. Other sites, social network platforms, and local groups have been formed and developed to support individuals' unique needs in very targeted ways. Love pets? There's a site for you. Want to find other quilters? There's a local group to meet with. Want to talk about agriculture? There's a weekly chat on Twitter about the topic; just follow the hashtag agchat.

I find in both my own research and many other writings that focus on the time in which we're living that people are seeking *authentic connection* and *a return to storytelling*. What they *don't* want is perfection, more commercialization, or a requirement to conform. They want to be understood for whom and where they are. They don't want advice; rather they seek firsthand knowledge of how to address a problem or issue or how to make a change from someone who has been there and is willing to talk about it authentically.

Less Control over Entry Point and Multichannel

Marketers will have to learn that although they can measure the payoff for their campaigns in the new world order, it won't be with the same level of immediacy as they have used before. I have heard many companies referring to their once-important home page as their largest landing page. They no longer have the control they once did over how and where the consumer is entering their website.

It takes time to establish a relationship with your end consumers and to understand where you stand with them in their current ecosystems. Instead of launching a campaign and looking for an immediate uptick, marketers must learn how to roll a campaign out gradually and measure its effectiveness over time. This will mean assessing various parts of the big data that you're collecting in better ways.

I liken the land grab for creating big data repositories to the land grabs of early America. The Dust Bowl of the 1930s—when American and Canadian prairie lands had been overworked, causing dust storms and droughts to ensue—came as a direct result of ignorance. Specifically, it came about because of people's failure to pay attention to how they should use their land. If companies do essentially the same thing with big data and use only their internal understanding and the patterns that emerge within what they collect, they will miss the mark on what the information means and how they should build products moving forward. Companies *must* use deep knowledge of their consumers to truly unlock the most crucial parts of the data being collected.

The Rising Phenomenon of the Unseen Brand

If you think about it, you realize that so much of what we buy now is unseen. We carry around digital devices that all look the same (except maybe for the case we choose to put on the outside). We're no longer able to tell what someone is reading, viewing, listening to, and playing on these devices. We often learn about this only by seeing what the individual might share or discuss on a social network.

This adds a level of complexity to the once-tangible process of gaining awareness for a product. One attempt I have seen a brand make is Kindle's built-in feature that allows readers to share a passage of a book or article that they have read across the reader's social media channels.

It's about Relationship

Begging a consumer to like you or share something without taking the time to understand why they would like what you have to offer—or how it benefits their core DNA—is a mistake of substantial proportions. It's today's equivalent of the obnoxious car commercials we are all familiar with that blares from the television screen, screaming "no money down" or "big sale." People have spent a lot of time debating the value of a like or tweet in recent years, focusing primarily on what happens at this point of interaction, not why it happened or why others truly participated.

The world of marketing and product management has been turned upside down. If you love change, it's a great time to be in this space. And if you don't . . . well, it's time to learn to love it.

The kind of marketing that focused on transactions must now focus on relationship. Sales is now the transactional part of the buyer's journey. Businesses need to revisit traditional company roles as they work to change their behaviors to align with the change in the consumer.

I know I have emphasized the analogy that brands, companies, and experiences must see themselves as a person. I also know that this is actually very difficult to do. And the larger the organization, the more difficult it becomes to act like an individual and modify behavior to fit the changing environment. Too many processes and claims of "We have done it this way for years" exist, even in companies that tout expertise in relationship-based marketing. Smaller companies are far more likely to succeed in this new paradigm. They must learn to listen to their consumer and resist the temptation to sell the consumer on their idea.

It's absolutely crucial to begin viewing your consumers in a very different way. You must take the time to find out why they buy your product, use your service, participate in an experience, or spend money on your brand. The companies that follow this new process of understanding their consumers and establishing trusted relationships will be the ones that will grow and prosper in our new mass customization economy—an economy that demands that you understand the individual *before* you do anything else.

As I said at the beginning of this book, it's one of the coolest times to be in marketing and product development. It's time to create new rules, new ways of doing business, and new methods for measuring success. And the very cool thing is that the secret to being successful in this endeavor simply requires that we do something that's so basic to each of us as human beings that we have forgotten how to do it: we just need to *understand one another*.

Index